Microsoft® Windows xp

Illustrated Essentials

Mary Kemper

COURSE
TECHNOLOGY

THOMSON LEARNING ™

Australia • Canada • Mexico • Singapore • Spain • United Kingdom • United States

COURSE TECHNOLOGY

™

THOMSON LEARNING

Microsoft® Windows XP—Illustrated Essentials

Mary Kemper

Managing Editor:
Nicole Jones Pinard

Product Manager:
Emily Heberlein

Associate Product Manager:
Christina Kling Garrett

Production Editor:
Danielle Power

Developmental Editor:
Lisa Ruffolo

Editorial Assistant:
Elizabeth M. Harris

QA Manuscript Reviewers:
Marianne Broughey,
Christian Kunciw

Text Designer:
Joseph Lee, Black Fish Design

Composition House:
GEX Publishing Services

The Illustrated Series Vision

Teaching and writing about computer applications can be extremely rewarding and challenging. How do we engage students and keep their interest? How do we teach them skills that they can easily apply on the job? As we set out to write this book, our goals were to develop a textbook that:

▶ works for a beginning student

▶ provides varied, flexible and meaningful exercises and projects to reinforce the skills

▶ serves as a reference tool

▶ makes your job as an educator easier, by providing resources above and beyond the textbook to help you teach your course

Our popular, streamlined format is based on advice from instructional designers and customers. This flexible design presents each lesson on a two-page spread, with step-by-step instructions on the left, and screen illustrations on the right. This signature style, coupled with high-caliber content, provides a comprehensive yet manageable introduction to Microsoft Windows XP - it is a teaching package for the instructor and a learning experience for the student.

AUTHOR ACKNOWLEDGMENTS

Thank you to Lisa Ruffolo for her quick and friendly editorial help on this book, to Emily Heberlein for her watchful managerial eye, especially as the book neared completion, and to John Bosco and his team of testers for their thorough search for errors. Thanks, as always, to Nicole Pinard and all the Illustrated Team for the opportunity to work on this great series of books. And most importantly, thanks to my husband, Steve, and our three little boys, Daniel, Joseph, and Robert, for supporting my efforts at the computer.

Mary Kemper

Preface

Welcome to *Microsoft Windows XP–Illustrated Essentials*. Each lesson in this book contains elements pictured to the right in the sample two-page spread.

▶ How is the book organized?
The book is organized into two units, covering basic Windows XP and file management skills. An appendix on formatting a disk is also included.

▶ What kinds of assignments are included in the book? At what level of difficulty?

- **Concepts Reviews** include multiple choice, matching, and screen identification questions.

- **Skills Reviews** provide additional hands-on, step-by-step reinforcement.

- **Independent Challenges** are case projects requiring critical thinking and application of the unit skills. The Independent Challenges increase in difficulty, with the first one in each unit being the easiest (most step-by-step with detailed instructions). Subsequent Independent Challenges become increasingly open-ended, requiring more independent problem solving.

- **Visual Workshops** show a completed file and require that the file be created without any step-by-step guidance, involving independent problem solving.

Each 2-page spread focuses on a single skill.

Concise text that introduces the basic principles discussed in the lesson.

Unit B

Windows XP

Working with Multiple Programs

A powerful feature of Windows is its capability to run more than one program at a time. For example, you might be working with a document in WordPad and want to search the Internet to find the answer to a question. You can start your browser, a program designed to access information on the Internet, without closing WordPad. When you find the information, you can leave your browser open and switch back to WordPad. Each open program is represented by a program button on the taskbar that you click to switch between programs. You can also copy data from one file to another (whether or not the files were created with the same Windows program) using the Clipboard, an area of memory on your computer's hard drive, and the Cut, Copy, and Paste commands. See Table B-2 for a description of these commands. ◀— In this lesson, you copy the logo graphic you worked with in the previous lesson into the memo you created in WordPad.

Steps

1. Click **Edit** on the menu bar, then click **Select All** to select the entire picture
   A dotted rectangle surrounds the picture, indicating it is selected, as shown in Figure B-5.

2. Click **Edit** on the menu bar, then click **Copy**
   The logo is copied to the Clipboard. When you copy an object onto the Clipboard, the object remains in its original location and is also available to be pasted into another location.

QuickTip
To switch between programs using the keyboard, press and hold down [Alt], press [Tab] until you select the program you want, then release [Alt].

3. Click the **WordPad program button** on the taskbar
   WordPad becomes the active program.

4. Click in the first line below the line that ends "for our company brochure."
   The insertion point indicates where the logo will be pasted.

5. Click the **Paste button** 🔲 on the WordPad toolbar
   The contents of the Clipboard, in this case the logo, are pasted into the WordPad file, as shown in Figure B-6.

6. Click the WordPad **Close button**; click **Yes** to save changes
   Your WordPad document and the WordPad program close. Paint is now the active program.

7. Click the Paint **Close button**; if you are prompted to save changes, click **Yes**
   Your Paint document and the Paint program close. You return to the desktop.

CLUES TO USE

Other Programs that Come with Windows XP

WordPad and Paint are just two of many programs that come with Windows XP. From the All Programs menu on the Start menu, you can access everything from games and entertainment programs to powerful communications software and disk maintenance programs without installing anything other than Windows XP. For example, from the Accessories menu, you can open a simple calculator; start Windows Movie Maker to create, edit, and share movie files; and use the Address Book to keep track of your contacts. From the Communications submenu, you can use NetMeeting to set up a voice and/or video conference over the Internet, or use the Remote Desktop Connection to allow another person to access your computer for diagnosing and solving computer problems. Several other menus and submenus display programs and tools that come with Windows XP. You can get a brief description of each by holding your mouse pointer over the name of the program in the menu. You might have to install some of these programs from the Windows CD if they don't appear on the menus.

▶ WINDOWS XP B-6 **WORKING WITH PROGRAMS, FILES, AND FOLDERS**

Hints as well as troubleshooting advice, right where you need it – next to the step itself.

Clues to Use boxes provide concise information that either expands on the major lesson skill or describes an independent task that in some way relates to the major lesson skill.

Clear step-by-step directions explain how to complete the specific task, with what students are to type in green.

Every lesson features large, full-color representations of what the screen should look like as students complete the numbered steps.

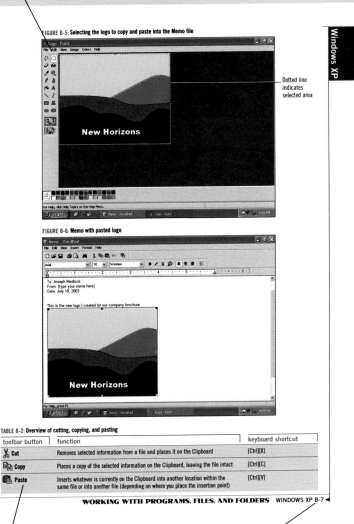

FIGURE B-5: Selecting the logo to copy and paste into the Memo file

Dotted line indicates selected area

New Horizons

FIGURE B-6: Memo with pasted logo

To: Joseph Medlock
From: [type your name here]
Date: July 18, 2003

This is the new logo I created for our company brochure.

New Horizons

TABLE B-2: Overview of cutting, copying, and pasting

toolbar button	function	keyboard shortcut
✂ Cut	Removes selected information from a file and places it on the Clipboard	[Ctrl][X]
📋 Copy	Places a copy of the selected information on the Clipboard, leaving the file intact	[Ctrl][C]
📋 Paste	Inserts whatever is currently on the Clipboard into another location within the same file or into another file (depending on where you place the insertion point)	[Ctrl][V]

WORKING WITH PROGRAMS, FILES, AND FOLDERS WINDOWS XP B-7 ◄

Quickly accessible summaries of key terms, toolbar buttons, or keyboard alternatives connected with the lesson material. Students can refer easily to this information when working on their own projects at a later time.

The pages are numbered according to unit. B indicates the unit, 7 indicates the page.

► What online learning options are available to accompany this book?

Visit www.course.com for more information on our Online Learning materials to accompany Illustrated titles. Options include:

WebCT

Course Technology and WebCT have partnered to provide you with the highest quality online resources and Web-based tools for your class. Course Technology offers content for this book to help you create your WebCT class, such as a suggested Syllabus, Lecture Notes, Practice Test questions, and more.

Blackboard

Course Technology and Blackboard have also partnered to provide you with the highest quality online resources and Web-based tools for your class. Course Technology offers content for this book to help you create your Blackboard class, such as a suggested Syllabus, Lecture Notes, Practice Test questions, and more.

Instructor Resources

The Instructor's Resource Kit (IRK) CD is Course Technology's way of putting the resources and information needed to teach and learn effectively into your hands. All the components are available on the IRK, (pictured below), and many of the resources can be downloaded from www.course.com.

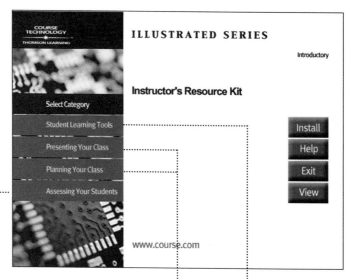

ASSESSING YOUR STUDENTS

Solution Files
Solution Files are Project Files completed with comprehensive sample answers. Use these files to evaluate your students' work. Or, distribute them electronically or in hard copy so students can verify their own work.

ExamView
ExamView is a powerful testing software package that allows you to create and administer printed, computer (LAN-based), and Internet exams. ExamView includes hundreds of questions that correspond to the topics covered in this text, enabling students to generate detailed study guides that include page references for further review. The computer-based and Internet testing components allow students to take exams at their computers, and also save you time by grading each exam automatically.

PRESENTING YOUR CLASS

Figure Files
Figure Files contain all the figures from the book in .bmp format. Use the figure files to create transparency masters or in a PowerPoint presentation.

STUDENT TOOLS

Project Files
To complete most of the units in this book, your students will need **Project Files**. Put them on a file server for students to copy. The Project Files are available on the Instructor's Resource Kit CD-ROM, the Review Pack, and can also be downloaded from www.course.com.

PLANNING YOUR CLASS

Instructor's Manual
Available as an electronic file, the Instructor's Manual is quality-assurance tested and includes unit overviews, detailed lecture topics for each unit with teaching tips, comprehensive sample solutions to all lessons and end-of-unit material, and Extra Independent Challenges. The Instructor's Manual is available on the Instructor's Resource Kit CD-ROM, or you can download it from www.course.com.

Sample Syllabus
Prepare and customize your course easily using this sample course outline (available on the Instructor's Resource Kit CD-ROM).

Contents

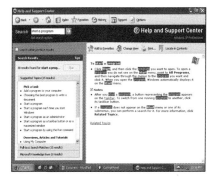

Read This Before You Begin

Software Information and Required Installation

This book was written to Microsoft Windows XP Professional, and quality-assurance tested on both Windows XP Professional and Windows XP Home. You can perform all the steps in this book using either the Professional or Home versions. Depending on whether you are using Home or Professional, and whether you have upgraded to Windows XP or are using a clean installation, your desktop may appear differently from the screen shots shown in the book.

What are Project Files?

To complete the steps in Unit B of this book, you will need to use Project Files. You use a Project File so you don't have to create all the files from scratch for each exercise. Your instructor will either provide you with a copy of the Project Files or ask you to make your own copy. Detailed instructions on how to download your Project Files from www.course.com are located on the inside back cover of this book.

If you plan to use floppy disks to complete the lessons and exercises in Unit B, you will need to have 2 blank, formatted floppy disks available. Create a label that says "Project Disk for Unit B" for the first disk. This Project Disk will be used to complete the lessons, Skills Review, and Independent Challenge 1. The Project Files you will need are:

> Win B-1.bmp
> Win B-2.bmp

The second disk will be used for Independent Challenge 2. Create a disk label that says "IC2" for the second disk. When instructed in the steps, use this disk when completing Independent Challenge 2.

Getting
Started with Windows XP

Objectives

- ► Start Windows and view the desktop
- ► Use the mouse
- ► Start a program
- ► Move and resize windows
- ► Use menus, keyboard shortcuts, and toolbars
- ► Use dialog boxes
- ► Use scroll bars
- ► Use Windows Help and Support Center
- ► Close a program and shut down Windows

Microsoft Windows XP, or simply Windows, is an operating system. An **operating system** is a kind of computer program that controls how a computer carries out basic tasks such as displaying information on your computer screen and running other programs. Windows helps you save and organize the results of your work as **files**, which are electronic collections of data, with each collection having a unique name (called the **filename**). Windows also coordinates the flow of information among the programs, printers, storage devices, and other components of your computer system, as well as among other computers on a network. When you work with Windows, you use **icons**, small pictures intended to be meaningful symbols of the items they represent. You will also use rectangular-shaped work areas known as windows, thus the name of the operating system. ✐— This unit introduces you to basic skills that you can use in all Windows programs.

Windows XP

Starting Windows and Viewing the Desktop

When you turn on your computer, Windows XP automatically starts and the desktop appears (you may be prompted to select your user name and/or enter your password first). The desktop, shown in Figure A-1, is where you can organize all the information and tools you need to accomplish your computer tasks. On the desktop, you can access, store, share, and explore information seamlessly, whether it resides on your computer, a network, or on the **Internet**, a worldwide collection of over 40 million computers linked together to share information. When you start Windows for the first time, the desktop appears with the **default** settings, those preset by the operating system. For example, the default color of the desktop is blue. If any of the default settings have been changed on your computer, your desktop will look different from the one in the figures, but you should be able to locate the items you need. The bar at the bottom of the screen is the **taskbar**, which shows what programs are currently running. You click the **Start button** at the left end of the taskbar to perform such tasks as starting programs, finding and opening files, and accessing Windows Help. The **Quick Launch toolbar** often appears next to the Start button; it contains several buttons you can click to start Internet-related programs quickly, and another that you can click to show the desktop when it is not currently visible. Table A-1 identifies the icons and other elements you see on your desktop. ➤ If Windows XP is not currently running on your computer, follow the steps below to start it now.

Steps

Trouble?

If a Welcome to Microsoft Windows tour opens, move your mouse pointer over the Next button in the lower-right corner of the dialog box and click the left mouse button once; when you see the Do you want to activate Windows now? dialog box, click the No, remind me every few days option. See your instructor or technical support person for further assistance.

1. Turn on your computer and monitor

When Windows starts, you may see an area where you can click your user name or a Log On to Windows dialog box. If so, continue to Step 2. If not, view Figure A-1, then continue on to the next lesson.

2. Click the correct user name, if necessary, type your password, then press **[Enter]**

Once the password is accepted, the Windows desktop appears on your screen. See Figure A-1. If you don't know your password, see your instructor or technical support person.

FIGURE A-1: Windows desktop

Icons (yours
might be
different)

Start button

Taskbar

Quick Launch
toolbar

Accessing the Internet from the Desktop

Windows XP provides a seamless connection between your desktop and the Internet with Internet Explorer. Internet Explorer is an example of a **browser**, a program designed to access the **World Wide Web** (also known as the **WWW**, or simply the **Web**). Internet Explorer is included with the Windows XP operating system. You can access it on the Start menu or by clicking its icon if it appears on the desktop or on the Quick Launch toolbar. You can use it to access Web pages and to place Web content such as weather or stock updates on the desktop for instant viewing. This information is updated automatically whenever you connect to the Internet.

TABLE A-1: Elements of a typical Windows desktop

desktop element	icon	allows you to
My Computer		Work with different disk drives, folders, and files on your computer
My Documents folder		Store documents, graphics, video and sound clips, and other files
Internet Explorer		Start the Internet Explorer browser to access the Internet
Recycle Bin		Delete and restore files
My Network Places		Open files and folders on other computers and install network printers
My Briefcase		Synchronize files when you use two computers
Outlook Express		Send and receive e-mail and participate in newsgroups
Start button		Start programs, open documents, search for files, and more
Taskbar		Start programs and switch among open programs and files
Quick Launch toolbar		Display the desktop, start Internet Explorer, and start Outlook Express

Windows XP

Using the Mouse

A **mouse** is a handheld **input** or **pointing device** that you use to interact with your computer. Input or pointing devices come in many shapes and sizes; some, like a mouse, are directly attached to your computer with a cable; others function like a TV remote control and allow you to access your computer without being right next to it. Figure A-2 shows examples of common pointing devices. Because the most common pointing device is a mouse, this book uses that term. If you are using a different pointing device, substitute that device whenever you see the term "mouse." When you move the mouse, the **mouse pointer** on the screen moves in the same direction. You use the **mouse buttons** to select icons and commands, which is how you communicate with the computer. Table A-2 shows some common mouse pointer shapes that indicate different activities. Table A-3 lists the five basic mouse actions. ➤ Begin by experimenting with the mouse now.

Steps

1. **Locate the mouse pointer on the desktop, then move the mouse across your desk or mouse pad**

   Watch how the mouse pointer moves on the desktop in response to your movements; practice moving the mouse pointer in circles, then back and forth in straight lines.

Trouble?

If the Recycle Bin window opens during this step, your mouse isn't set with the Windows XP default mouse settings. See your instructor or technical support person for assistance. This book assumes your computer is set to all Windows XP default settings.

2. **Position the mouse pointer over the Recycle Bin icon** 🗑

   Positioning the mouse pointer over an item is called **pointing**.

3. **With the pointer over the** 🗑**, press and release the left mouse button**

   Pressing and releasing the left mouse button is called **clicking** (or single-clicking, to distinguish it from double-clicking, which you'll do in Step 7). When you position the mouse pointer over an icon or any item and click, you select that item. When an item is **selected,** it is **highlighted** (shaded differently from other items), and the next action you take will be performed on that item.

4. **With** 🗑 **selected, press and hold down the left mouse button, move the mouse down and to the right, then release the mouse button**

   The icon becomes dimmed and moves with the mouse pointer; this is called **dragging**, which you do to move icons and other Windows elements. When you release the mouse button, the item is positioned at the new location (it may "snap" to another location, depending on the settings on your computer).

5. **Position the mouse pointer over the** 🗑**, then press and release the right mouse button**

   Clicking the right mouse button is known as **right-clicking**. Right-clicking an item on the desktop produces a **shortcut menu**, as shown in Figure A-3. This menu lists the commands most commonly used for the item you have clicked. A **command** is a directive that provides access to a program's features.

QuickTip

When a step tells you to "click," use the left mouse button. If it says "right-click," use the right mouse button.

6. **Click anywhere outside the menu to close the shortcut menu**

7. **Position the mouse pointer over the** 🗑**, then quickly press and release the left mouse button twice**

   Clicking the mouse button twice quickly is known as **double-clicking**; in this case, double-clicking the Recycle Bin icon opens the Recycle Bin window, which displays files that you have deleted.

8. **Click the Close button** ☒ **in the upper-right corner of the Recycle Bin window**

FIGURE A-2: Common pointing devices

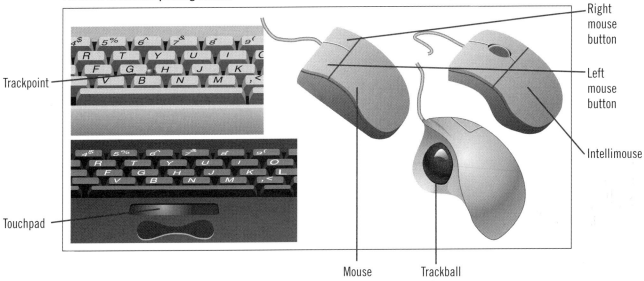

Trackpoint

Touchpad

Right mouse button

Left mouse button

Intellimouse

Mouse   Trackball

FIGURE A-3: Displaying a shortcut menu

Pointer positioned over icon

Selected icon

Shortcut menu

Open
Explore
Empty Recycle Bin
Create Shortcut
Properties

TABLE A-2: Common mouse pointer shapes

shape	used to
⇗	Select items, choose commands, start programs, and work in programs
I	Position mouse pointer for editing or inserting text; called the insertion point or Text Select pointer
⧖	Indicate Windows is busy processing a command
↔	Change the size of a window; appears when mouse pointer is on the border of a window
⇧	Select and open Web-based data and other links

TABLE A-3: Basic mouse techniques

technique	what to do
Pointing	Move the mouse to position the mouse pointer over an item on the desktop
Clicking	Press and release the left mouse button
Double-clicking	Press and release the left mouse button twice quickly
Dragging	Point to an item, press and hold the left mouse button, move the mouse to a new location, then release the mouse button
Right-clicking	Point to an item, then press and release the right mouse button

Windows XP

Starting a Program

Clicking the Start button on the taskbar opens the **Start menu**, which lists submenus for a variety of tasks described in Table A-4. As you become familiar with Windows, you might want to customize the Start menu to include additional items that you use most often. Windows XP comes with several built-in programs, called **accessories**. Although not as feature-rich as many programs sold separately, Windows accessories are useful for completing basic tasks. ➤ In this lesson, you start a Windows accessory called **WordPad**, which is a word-processing program you can use to create and edit simple documents.

1. Click the **Start button** on the taskbar
The Start menu opens.

2. Point to **All Programs**
The All Programs submenu opens, listing the programs and categories for programs installed on your computer. WordPad is in the category called Accessories.

QuickTip

The left side of the Windows XP Start menu lists programs you've used recently, so the next time you want to open WordPad, most likely it will be handy in this list of recently opened programs.

3. Point to **Accessories**
The Accessories menu, shown in Figure A-4, contains several programs to help you complete common tasks. You want to start WordPad.

4. Click **WordPad**
WordPad starts and opens a blank document window, as shown in Figure A-5. Don't worry if your window does not fill the screen; you'll learn how to maximize it in the next lesson. Note that a program button appears on the taskbar and is highlighted, indicating that WordPad is open.

TABLE A-4: Start menu categories

category	description
Default	Displays the name of the current user; different users can customize the Start menu to fit their work habits
Internet Explorer / Outlook Express	The two programs many people use for a browser and e-mail program; you can add programs you use often to this list (called the "pinned items list")
Frequently used programs list	Located below Internet Explorer and Outlook Express, contains the last six programs used on your computer; you can change the number listed
All Programs	Displays a menu of most programs installed on your computer
My Documents, etc.	The five items in this list allow you to quickly access files you've saved in the three folders listed (My Documents, My Pictures, and My Music), as well as access My Computer, which you use to manage files, folders, and drives on your computer; the My Recent Documents list contains the last 15 files that have been opened on your computer
Control Panel / Connect To / Printers and Faxes	Control Panel displays tools for selecting settings on your computer; Connect To lists Internet connections that have been set up on your computer; and Printers and Faxes lists the printers and faxes connected to your computer
Help and Support / Search / Run	Help and Support provides access to Help topics and other support services; Search locates files, folders, computers on your network, and Web pages on the Internet; Run opens a program, file, or Web site by letting you type commands or names in a dialog box
Log Off / Turn Off Computer	End your Windows session; used when you are done using the computer and don't expect to use it again soon

FIGURE A-4: Cascading menus

Arrow indicates submenu

Click to open WordPad

Submenu

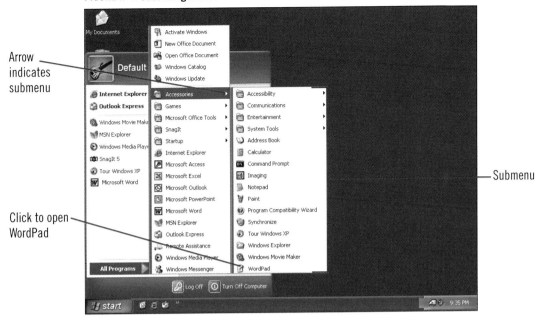

FIGURE A-5: WordPad program window

Document window

Program button indicates open program

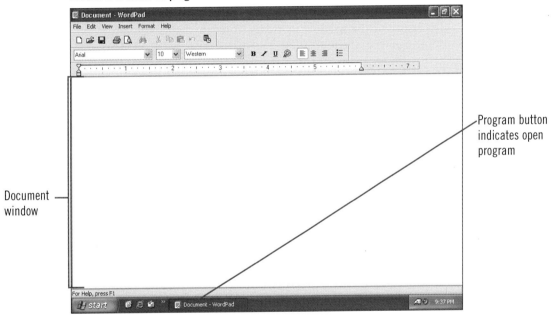

Customizing the Start Menu

With Windows XP, you can change the way the Start menu looks and behaves by opening the Control Panel (click the Start button and then click Control Panel), switching to Classic view, if necessary, then double-clicking Taskbar and Start Menu. To get the look and feel of the classic Start menu from earlier versions of Windows, click the Start Menu tab and then click the Classic Start menu option button. You can then click the Customize button to add shortcuts to the Start menu for desired programs and documents, or change the order in which they appear. To preserve the Windows XP look of the Start menu but modify how it behaves, click the Customize button next to the Start menu and select the options you want.

Moving and Resizing Windows

One of the powerful features of Windows is the ability to open more than one window or program at once. This means, however, that the desktop can get cluttered with the various programs and files you are using. You can keep your desktop organized by changing the size of a window or moving it. You can do this by clicking the sizing buttons in the upper-right corner of any window or by dragging a corner or border of any window that does not completely fill the screen. Practice sizing and moving the WordPad window now.

Steps

1. **If the WordPad window does not already fill the screen, click the Maximize button ▣ in the WordPad window**
   When a window is **maximized**, it takes up the whole screen.

2. **Click the Restore button ▣ in the WordPad window**
   To **restore** a window is to return it to its previous size, as shown in Figure A-6. The Restore button only appears when a window is maximized.

3. **Position the pointer on the right edge of the WordPad window until the pointer changes to ↔, then drag the border to the right**
   The width of the window increases. You can change the height or width of a window by dragging any of the four sides.

   > **QuickTip**
   > You can resize windows by dragging any corner. You can also drag any border to make the window taller, shorter, wider, or narrower.

4. **Position the pointer in the lower-right corner of the WordPad window until the pointer changes to ↘, as shown in Figure A-6, then drag down and to the right**
   The height and width of the window increase proportionally when you drag a corner instead of a side. You can also position a restored window wherever you want on the desktop by dragging its title bar. The **title bar** is the area along the top of the window that displays the filename and program used to create it.

5. **Drag the title bar on the WordPad window up and to the left, as shown in Figure A-6**
   The window is repositioned on the desktop. At times, you might want to close a program window, yet keep the program running and easily accessible. You can accomplish this by minimizing a window.

   > **QuickTip**
   > If you have more than one window open and you want to quickly access something on the desktop, you can click the Show Desktop button 🗗 on the Quick Launch toolbar. All open windows are minimized so the desktop is visible. If your Quick Launch toolbar isn't visible, right-click the taskbar, point to Toolbars, and then click Quick Launch.

6. **In the WordPad window, click the Minimize button ▬**
   When you **minimize** a window, it shrinks to a program button on the taskbar, as shown in Figure A-7. WordPad is still running, but it is out of your way.

7. **Click the WordPad program button on the taskbar to reopen the window**
   The WordPad program window reopens.

8. **Click the Maximize button ▣ in the upper-right corner of the WordPad window**
   The window fills the screen.

FIGURE A-6: Restored program window

Title bar —

Sizing buttons

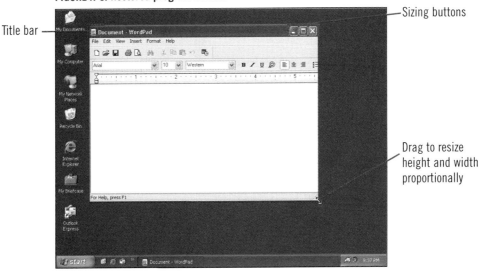

Drag to resize
height and width
proportionally

FIGURE A-7: Minimized program window

Indicates program
is running but
not in use

More about sizing windows

Keep in mind that some programs contain two sets of sizing buttons: one that controls the program window itself and another that controls the window for the file with which you are working. The program sizing buttons are located in the title bar and the file sizing buttons are located below them. See Figure A-8. When you minimize a file window within a program, the file window is reduced to an icon in the lower-left corner of the program window, but the size of the program window remains intact. (*Note:* WordPad does not use a second set of window sizing buttons.)

Also, to see the contents of more than one window at a time, you can open the desired windows, right-click a blank area on the taskbar, and then click either Tile Windows Vertically or Tile Windows Horizontally. With the former, you see the windows side by side, and with the latter, the windows are stacked one above the other. You can also click Cascade Windows to layer any open windows in the upper-left corner of the desktop, with the title bar of each clearly visible.

FIGURE A-8: Program and file sizing buttons

Program
window sizing
buttons

File window
sizing buttons

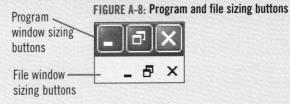

Windows XP

Using Menus, Keyboard Shortcuts, and Toolbars

A **menu** is a list of commands that you use to accomplish certain tasks. Each Windows program also has its own set of menus, which are located on the **menu bar** under the title bar. The menus organize commands into groups of related tasks. See Table A-5 for a description of items on a typical menu. **Toolbar buttons** offer another method for executing menu commands; instead of clicking the menu and then the menu command, you click the button for the command. A **toolbar** is a set of buttons usually positioned below the menu bar. ✎ You will open My Computer, use a menu and toolbar button to change how the contents of the window appear, and then add and remove a toolbar button.

Trouble?

If you don't see the My Computer icon on your desktop, right-click the desktop, click Properties, click the Desktop tab, click the Customize Desktop button, click the My Computer check box, then click OK twice.

1. Minimize WordPad, if necessary, then double-click the **My Computer icon** 🖳 on the desktop

   The My Computer window opens. You now have two windows open: WordPad and My Computer. My Computer is the **active window** (or active program) because it is the one with which you are currently working. WordPad is **inactive** because it is open but you are not working with it.

2. Click **View** on the menu bar

   The View menu appears, listing the View commands, as shown in Figure A-9. On a menu, a **check mark** identifies a feature that is currently enabled or "on." To disable or turn "off" the feature, you click the command again to remove the check mark. A **bullet mark** can also indicate that an option is enabled.

3. Click **List**

   The icons are now listed one after the other rather than as larger icons.

Trouble?

[Alt][V] means that you should press and hold down the Alt key, press the V key, and then release both simultaneously.

4. Press **[Alt][V]** to open the View menu, then press **[T]** to open the Toolbars submenu

   The View menu appears again, and then the Toolbars submenu appears, with check marks next to the selected commands. Notice that a letter in each command on the View menu is underlined. These are **keyboard navigation indicators**, indicating that you can press the underlined letter, known as a **keyboard shortcut**, instead of clicking to execute the command.

5. Press **[C]** to execute the Customize command

   The Customize Toolbar dialog box opens. A **dialog box** is a window in which you specify how you want to perform a task; you'll learn more about working in a dialog box shortly. In the Customize Toolbar dialog box, you can add toolbar buttons to the current toolbar, or remove buttons already on the toolbar. The list on the right shows which buttons are currently on the toolbar, and the list on the left shows which buttons are available to add.

6. Click the **Home button** in the Available toolbar buttons section, then click the **Add button** (located between the two lists)

   As shown in Figure A-10, the Home button is added to the Standard toolbar.

7. Click the **Home button** in the Current toolbar buttons section, click the **Remove button**, then click **Close** on the Customize Toolbar dialog box

   The Home button disappears from the Standard toolbar, and the Customize Toolbar dialog box closes.

QuickTip

When you rest the pointer over a button without clicking, a ScreenTip often appears with the button's name.

8. On the My Computer toolbar, click the **Views button list arrow** ▦▾, then click **Details**

   Some toolbar buttons have an arrow, which indicates the button contains several choices. Clicking the button shows the choices. The Details view includes a description of each item in the My Computer window.

FIGURE A-9: Opening a menu

Menu bar

Bullet

Commands in
View menu

Arrow indicates
submenu

Check mark

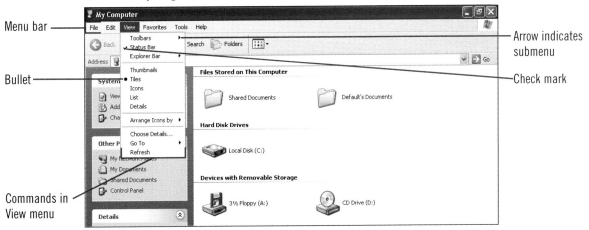

FIGURE A-10: Customize Toolbar dialog box

Click to move
selected button
to toolbar

Buttons you
can add to
the toolbar

Home button is
added to toolbar

Home button
listed here,
indicating it is
currently on the
toolbar

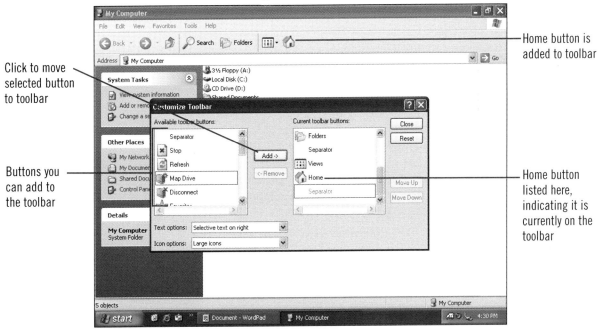

TABLE A-5: Typical items on a menu

item	description	example
Dimmed command	Indicates the menu command is not currently available	Recent File
Ellipsis	Indicates that a dialog box will open that allows you to select additional options	Save As...
Triangle	Opens a cascading menu containing an additional list of commands	Toolbars ▶
Keyboard shortcut	Executes a command using the keyboard instead of the mouse	Print... Ctrl+P
Underlined letter	Indicates the letter to press for the keyboard shortcut	Exit

Windows XP

Using Dialog Boxes

A **dialog box** is a window that opens when you choose a menu command that needs more information before the program can carry out the command you selected. Dialog boxes open in other situations as well, such as when you open a program in the Control Panel. See Figure A-11 and Table A-6 for some of the typical elements of a dialog box. Practice using a dialog box to control your mouse settings.

Trouble?

If you don't see Printers and Other Hardware in the Control Panel window, you are using Classic view, not the default Category view. In the left pane, click Switch to Category view.

1. **In the left side of the My Computer window, click Control Panel; in the Control Panel window, click Printers and Other Hardware, then click the Mouse icon** 🐭
The Mouse Properties dialog box opens, as shown in Figure A-12. **Properties** are characteristics of a computer element (in this case, the mouse) that you can customize. The options in this dialog box allow you to control the way the mouse buttons are configured, select the types of pointers that appear, choose the speed and behavior of the mouse movement on the screen, and specify what type of mouse you are using. **Tabs** at the top of the dialog box separate these options into related categories.

2. **Click the Pointer Options tab if necessary to make it the frontmost tab**
This tab contains three options for controlling the way your mouse moves. Under Motion, you can set how fast the pointer moves on the screen in relation to how you move the mouse. You drag a **slider** to specify how fast the pointer moves. Under Snap To is a **check box**, which is a toggle for turning a feature on or off—in this case, for setting whether you want your mouse pointer to move to the default button in dialog boxes. Under Visibility, you can choose three options for easily finding your cursor and keeping it out of the way when you're typing.

3. **Under Motion, drag the slider all the way to the left for Slow, then move the mouse pointer across your screen**
Notice how slowly the mouse pointer moves. After you select the options you want in a dialog box, you need to click a **command button**, which carries out the options you've selected. The two most common command buttons are OK and Cancel. Clicking OK accepts your changes and closes the dialog box; clicking Cancel leaves the original settings intact and closes the dialog box. The third command button in this dialog box is Apply. Clicking the Apply button accepts the changes you've made and keeps the dialog box open so that you can select additional options. Because you might share this computer with others, you should close the dialog box without making any permanent changes.

QuickTip

You can also use the keyboard to carry out commands in a dialog box. Pressing [Enter] is the same as clicking OK; pressing [Esc] is the same as clicking Cancel.

4. **Click Cancel**
The original settings remain intact, the dialog box closes, and you return to the Printers and Other Hardware window.

FIGURE A-11: Elements of a typical dialog box

Text box

Check box

Option buttons

Spin box

Command button

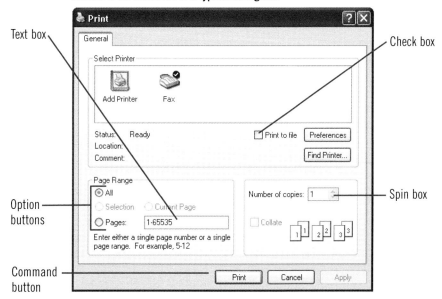

FIGURE A-12: Mouse Properties dialog box

Tabs

Slider

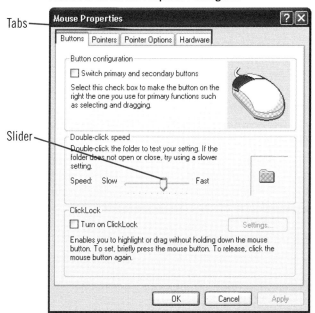

TABLE A-6: Typical items in a dialog box

item	description
Tab	A place in a dialog box that organizes related commands and options
Check box	A box that turns an option on (when the box is checked) and off (when it is unchecked)
Command button	A rectangular button with the name of the command on it
List box	A box containing a list of items; to choose an item, click the list arrow, then click the desired item
Option button	A small circle that you click to select a single dialog box option; you cannot select more than one option button in a list
Text box	A box in which you type text
Slider	A shape that you drag to set the degree to which an option is in effect
Spin box	A box with two arrows and a text box; allows you to scroll in numerical increments or type a number

Windows XP

Using Scroll Bars

When you cannot see all of the items available in a window, scroll bars appear on the right and/or bottom edges of the window. **Scroll bars** are the vertical and horizontal bars along the right and bottom edges of a window and contain elements that you click and drag so you can view the additional contents of the window. When you need to scroll only a short distance, you can use the scroll arrows. To scroll the window in larger increments, click in the scroll bar above or below the scroll box. Dragging the scroll box moves you quickly to a new part of the window. See Table A-7 for a summary of the different ways to use scroll bars. ✏ With the Control Panel window in Details view, you can use the scroll bars to view all of the items in this window.

Trouble?

Your window might be called Printers and Faxes or something similar, and the Printing link may appear as Troubleshoot printing, but you should still be able to complete the steps.

1. In the left side of the Printers and Other Hardware window, under Troubleshooters, click **Printing**

The Help and Support Center window opens, which you'll work with further in the next lesson. For now, you'll use the window to practice using the scroll bars.

2. If the Help and Support Center window fills the screen, click the **Restore button** 🗗 in the upper-right corner so the scroll bars appear, as shown in Figure A-13

Trouble?

If you don't see scroll bars, drag the lower-right corner of the Help and Support Center window up and to the left until scroll bars appear.

3. Click the **down scroll arrow**, as shown in Figure A-13

Clicking this arrow moves the view down one line.

4. Click the **up scroll arrow** in the vertical scroll bar

Clicking this arrow moves the view up one line.

5. Click anywhere in the area below the scroll box in the vertical scroll bar

The view moves down one window's height. Similarly, you can click in the scroll bar above the scroll box to move up one window's height. The size of the scroll box changes to reflect how much information does not fit in the window. A larger scroll box indicates that a relatively small amount of the window's contents is not currently visible; you need to scroll only a short distance to see the remaining items. A smaller scroll box indicates that a relatively large amount of information is currently not visible.

6. Drag the **scroll box** all the way up to the top of the vertical scroll bar

This view shows the items that appear at the top of the window.

7. In the horizontal scroll bar, click the area to the right of the scroll box

The far right edge of the window comes into view. The horizontal scroll bar works the same as the vertical scroll bar.

8. Click the area to the left of the scroll box in the horizontal scroll bar

9. Click the **Close button** ☒ to close the Help and Support Center window

You'll reopen the Help and Support Center window from the Start menu in the next lesson.

FIGURE A-13: Scroll bars

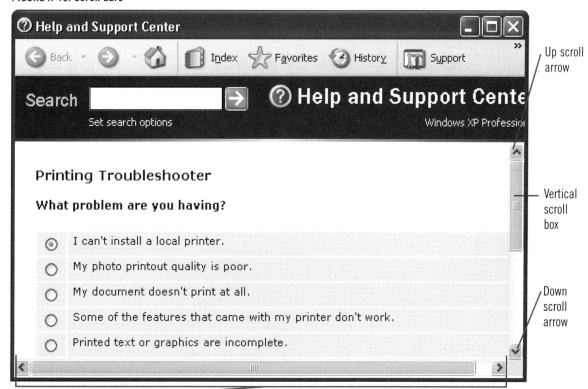

Horizontal scroll bar

TABLE A-7: Using scroll bars

to	do this
Move down one line	Click the down arrow at the bottom of the vertical scroll bar
Move up one line	Click the up arrow at the top of the vertical scroll bar
Move down one window height	Click in the area below the scroll box in the vertical scroll bar
Move up one window height	Click in the area above the scroll box in the vertical scroll bar
Move up a large distance in the window	Drag the scroll box up in the vertical scroll bar
Move down a large distance in the window	Drag the scroll box down in the vertical scroll bar
Move a short distance side-to-side in a window	Click the left or right arrows in the horizontal scroll bar
Move to the right one window width	Click in the area to the right of the scroll box in the horizontal scroll bar
Move to the left one window width	Click in the area to the left of the scroll box in the horizontal scroll bar
Move left or right a large distance in the window	Drag the scroll box in the horizontal scroll bar

Using Windows Help and Support Center

When you have a question about how to do something in Windows XP, you can usually find the answer with a few clicks of your mouse. The Windows Help and Support Center works like a book stored on your computer, with a table of contents and an index to make finding information easier. Help provides guidance on many Windows features, including detailed steps for completing procedures, definitions of terms, lists of related topics, and search capabilities. You can browse or search for information in the Help and Support Center window, or you can connect to a Microsoft Web site on the Internet for the latest technical support on Windows XP. You can also access **context-sensitive help**, help specifically related to what you are doing, using a variety of methods such as holding your mouse pointer over an item or using the question mark button in a dialog box. In this lesson, you get Help on starting a program. You also get information about the taskbar.

Steps

1. **Click the Start button on the taskbar, click Help and Support, then click the Maximize button** ☐ **if the window doesn't fill the screen**
   The Help and Support Center window opens, as shown in Figure A-14. This window has a toolbar at the top of the window, a Search box below where you enter keywords having to do with your question, a left pane where the items matching your keywords are listed, and a right pane where the specific steps for a given item are listed.

2. **Click in the Search text box, type start a program, press [Enter], then view the Help topics displayed in the left pane**
   The left pane contains a selection of topics related to starting a program. The Suggested Topics are the most likely matches for your search text.

3. **Click Start a program**
   Help information for this topic appears in the right pane, as shown in Figure A-15. At the bottom of the text in the right pane, you can click Related Topics to view a list of topics that are related to the current topic. Some Help topics also allow you to view additional information about important words; these words are underlined, indicating that you can click them to display a pop-up window with the additional information.

4. **Click the underlined word taskbar, read the definition, then click anywhere outside the pop-up window to close it**

5. **On the toolbar at the top of the window, click the Index button**
   The Index provides an alphabetical list of all the available Help topics, like an index at the end of a book. You can type a topic in the text box at the top of the pane. You can also scroll down to the topic. In either case, you click the topic you're interested in and the details about that topic appear in the right pane.

6. **In the left pane, type tiling windows**
   As you type, the list of topics automatically scrolls to try to match the word or phrase you type.

7. **Double-click tiling windows in the list in the left pane and read the steps and notes in the right pane**
   You can also click the Related Topics link for more information.

8. **Click the Support button on the toolbar**
   Information on the Web sites for Windows XP Help appears in the right pane (a **Web site** is a document or related documents that contain highlighted words, phrases, and graphics that link to other sites on the Internet). To access online support or information, you would click one of the available options in the left pane.

9. **Click the Close button** ☒ **in the upper-right corner of the Help and Support Center window**
   The Help and Support Center window closes.

FIGURE A-14: Windows Help and Support Center

Help toolbar

Type keyword or phrase to search for topics

Links for popular Help topics

FIGURE A-15: Viewing a Help topic

Type search text here

Left pane contains list of Help topics matching your search text

Click this topic

Right pane contains information on the topic you select

Other forms of Help

The Help and Support Center offers information on Windows itself, not on all the other programs you can run on your computer. To get help on a specific Windows program, click Help on that program's menu bar. Also, to receive help in a dialog box (whether you are in Windows or another program), click the Help button ? in the upper-right corner of the dialog box; the mouse pointer changes to ?. Click any item in the dialog box that you want to learn more about. If information is available on that item, a pop-up window appears with a brief explanation of the selected feature.

Windows XP

Closing a Program and Shutting Down Windows

When you are finished working on your computer, you need to make sure you shut it down properly. This involves several steps: saving and closing all open files, closing all the open programs and windows, shutting down Windows, and finally, turning off the computer. If you turn off the computer while Windows is running, you could lose important data. To **close** a program, you can click the Close button in the window's upper-right corner or click File on the menu bar and choose either Close or Exit. To shut down Windows after all your files and programs are closed, click Turn Off Computer on the Start menu, then select the desired option in the Turn off computer dialog box, shown in Figure A-16. See Table A-8 for a description of shut down options. ◣━━ Close all your open files, windows, and programs, then exit Windows.

1. In the Control Panel window, click the **Close button** ⊠ in the upper-right corner of the window
   The Control Panel window closes.

2. Click **File** on the WordPad menu bar, then click **Exit**
   If you have made any changes to the open file, you will be asked to save your changes before the program closes. Some programs also give you the option of choosing the Close command on the File menu in order to close the active file but leave the program open, so you can continue to work in it with a different file. Also, if there is a second set of sizing buttons in the window, the Close button on the menu bar will close the active file only, leaving the program open for continued use.

3. If you see a message asking you to save changes to the document, click **No**
   WordPad closes and you return to the desktop.

QuickTip

Complete the remaining steps to shut down Windows and your computer only if you have been told to do so by your instructor or technical support person. If you have been told to Log Off instead of exiting Windows, click Log Off instead of Turn Off Computer, and follow the directions from your instructor or technical support person.

4. Click the **Start button** on the taskbar, then click **Turn Off Computer**
   The Turn off computer dialog box opens, as shown in Figure A-16. In this dialog box, you have the option to stand by, turn off the computer, or restart the computer.

5. If you are working in a lab, click **Cancel** to leave the computer running; if you are working on your own machine or if your instructor told you to shut down Windows, click **Turn Off**, then click **OK**

6. If you see the message "It is now safe to turn off your computer," turn off your computer and monitor
   On some computers, the power shuts off automatically, so you may not see this message.

FIGURE A-16: Turn off computer dialog box

Click to leave Windows running but reduce computer's power mode

Click to exit Windows and automatically restart it

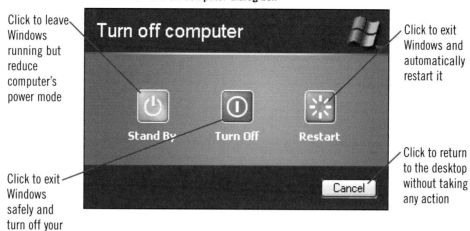

Click to exit Windows safely and turn off your computer

Click to return to the desktop without taking any action

The Log Off command

To change users on the same computer quickly, you can choose the Log Off command from the Start menu. When you click this command, you can choose to switch users, so that the current user is logged off and another user can log on, or you can simply log off. Windows XP shuts down partially, stopping at the point where you click your user name. When you or a new user clicks a user name (and enters a password, if necessary), Windows restarts and the desktop appears as usual.

TABLE A-8: Turn off options

Turn off option	function	when to use it
Stand By	Leaves Windows running but on minimal power	When you are finished working with Windows for a short time and plan to return before the end of the day
Turn Off	Exits Windows completely and safely	When you are finished working with Windows and want to shut off your computer for an extended time (such as overnight or longer)
Restart	Exits Windows safely, turns off the computer automatically, and then restarts the computer and Windows	When your programs might have frozen or stopped working correctly

Practice

► Concepts Review

Identify each of the items labeled in Figure A-17.

FIGURE A-17

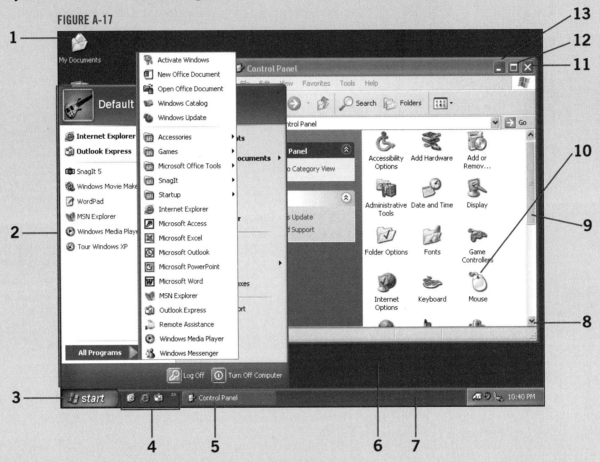

Match each of the statements with the term it describes.

14. Shrinks a window to a button on the taskbar
15. Shows the name of the window or program
16. The taskbar item you first click to start a program
17. Requests more information for you to supply before carrying out command
18. Shows the Start button, Quick Launch toolbar, and any currently open programs
19. An input device that lets you point to and make selections
20. Graphic representation of program

a. dialog box
b. program button
c. taskbar
d. Minimize button
e. icon
f. mouse
g. Start button

Select the best answer from the list of choices.

21. The term "file" is best defined as
   a. a set of instructions for a computer to carry out a task.   c. a collection of icons.
   b. an electronic collection of data.   d. an international collection of computers.

22. **Which of the following is NOT provided by Windows XP?**
    a. The ability to organize files
    b. Instructions to coordinate the flow of information among the programs, files, printers, storage devices, and other components of your computer system
    c. Programs that allow you to specify the operation of the mouse
    d. Spell checker for your documents

23. **All of the following are examples of using a mouse, EXCEPT**
    a. clicking the Maximize button.
    b. pressing [Enter].
    c. double-clicking to start a program.
    d. dragging the My Computer icon.

24. **The term for moving an item to a new location on the desktop is**
    a. pointing.
    b. clicking.
    c. dragging.
    d. restoring.

25. **The Maximize button is used to**
    a. return a window to its previous size.
    b. expand a window to fill the computer screen.
    c. scroll slowly through a window.
    d. run programs from the Start menu.

26. **What appears if a window contains more information than can be viewed in the window?**
    a. Program icon
    b. Cascading menu
    c. Scroll bars
    d. Check boxes

27. **A window is active when**
    a. you can only see its program button on the taskbar.
    b. its title bar is dimmed.
    c. it is open and you are currently using it.
    d. it is listed in the Programs submenu.

28. **You can exit Windows by**
    a. double-clicking the Control Panel application.
    b. double-clicking the Program Manager control menu box.
    c. clicking File, then clicking Exit.
    d. selecting the Turn Off Computer command from the Start menu.

► Skills Review

1. **Start Windows and view the desktop.**
   a. Turn on the computer, select your user name, then enter a password, if necessary.
   b. After Windows starts, identify as many items on the desktop as you can, without referring to the lesson material.
   c. Compare your results to Figure A-1.

2. **Use the mouse.**
   a. Double-click the Recycle Bin icon, then click the Restore button if the window fills the screen.
   b. Drag the Recycle Bin window to the upper-right corner of the desktop.
   c. Right-click the title bar of the Recycle Bin, then click Close.

3. **Start a program.**
   a. Click the Start button on the taskbar, then point to All Programs.
   b. Point to Accessories, then click Calculator.
   c. Minimize the Calculator window.

4. **Move and resize windows.**
   a. Drag the Recycle Bin icon to the top of the desktop.
   b. Double-click the My Computer icon to open the My Computer window (if you don't see the My Computer icon, read the Trouble in the lesson on menus and toolbars for how to display it).
   c. Maximize the My Computer window, if it is not already maximized.
   d. Restore the window to its previous size.

   e. Resize the window until you see the vertical scroll bar.

   f. Minimize the My Computer window.

   g. Drag the Recycle Bin icon back to its original position.

5. Use menus, keyboard shortcuts, and toolbars.

   a. Click the Start button on the taskbar, then click Control Panel.

   b. Click View on the menu bar, point to Toolbars, then click Standard Buttons to deselect the option and hide the toolbar.

   c. Redisplay the toolbar.

   d. Press [Alt][V] to display the View menu, then press [B] to hide the status bar at the bottom of the window.

   e. Note the change, then use keyboard shortcuts to change the view back.

   f. Click the Up button to view My Computer.

   g. Click the Back button to return to the Control Panel.

   h. Click View, point to Toolbars, then click Customize.

   i. Add a button to the toolbar, remove it, then close the Customize Toolbar dialog box.

6. Use dialog boxes.

   a. With the Control Panel in Category view, click Appearance and Themes, click Display, then click the Screen Saver tab.

   b. Click the Screen saver list arrow, click any screen saver in the list, then view it in the preview monitor above the list.

   c. Click the Appearance tab in the Display Properties dialog box, then click the Effects button.

   d. In the Effects dialog box, click the Use large icons check box to select it, click the OK button to close the Effects dialog box, then click OK to close the Display Properties dialog box.

   e. Note the change in the icons on the desktop, minimizing windows if necessary.

   f. Right-click a blank area on the desktop, click Properties on the shortcut menu, click the Appearance tab, click the Effects button, click the Use large icons check box to deselect it, click OK, click the Screen Saver tab, return the screen saver to its original setting, then click Apply.

   g. Click the OK button in the Display Properties dialog box, but leave the Control Panel open and make it the active program.

7. Use scroll bars.

   a. In the left side of the Control Panel window, click Switch to Classic View, if necessary, click the Views button on the toolbar, then click Details.

   b. Drag the vertical scroll box down all the way.

   c. Click anywhere in the area above the vertical scroll box.

   d. Click the down scroll arrow until the scroll box is back at the bottom of the scroll bar.

   e. Click the right scroll arrow twice.

   f. Click in the area to the right of the horizontal scroll box.

   g. Drag the horizontal scroll box all the way back to the left.

8. Get Help.

   a. Click the Start button on the taskbar, then click Help and Support.

   b. Click Windows basics under Pick a Help topic, then click Tips for using Help in the left pane.

   c. In the right pane, click Add a Help topic or page to the Help and Support Center Favorites list.

   d. Read the topic contents, click Related Topics, click Print a Help topic or page, then read the contents. Leave the Help and Support Center open.

9. Close a program and shut down Windows.

   a. Click the Close button to close the Help and Support Center window.

   b. Click File on the menu bar, then click Close to close the Control Panel window.

   c. Click the Calculator program button on the taskbar to restore the window.

   d. Click the Close button in the Calculator window to close the Calculator program.

   e. If you are instructed to do so, shut down Windows and turn off your computer.

► Independent Challenge 1

You can use the Help and Support Center to learn more about Windows XP and explore Help on the Internet.

- **a.** Open the Help and Support Center window and locate help topics on adjusting the double-click speed of your mouse and displaying Web content on your desktop.
  If you have a printer, print a Help topic for each subject. Otherwise, write a summary of each topic.
- **b.** Follow these steps below to access help on the Internet. If you don't have Internet access, you can't do this step.
  - i.   Click a link under "Did you know?" in the right pane of the Help and Support Home page.
  - ii. In the left pane of the Microsoft Web page, click Using Windows XP, click How-to Articles, then click any link.
  - iii. Read the article, then write a summary of what you find.
  - iv. Click the browser's Close button, disconnect from the Internet, and close Help and Support Center.

► Independent Challenge 2

You can change the format and the actual time of the clock and date on your computer.

- **a.** Open the Control Panel window; in Category view, click Date, Time, Language, and Regional Options; click Regional and Language Options; then click the Customize button under Standards and formats.
- **b.** Click the Time tab, click the Time format list arrow, click H:mm:ss to change the time to show a 24-hour clock, then click the Apply button to view the changes, if any.
- **c.** Click the Date tab, click the Short date format list arrow, click dd-MMM-yy, then click the Apply button.
- **d.** Click the Cancel button twice to close the open dialog boxes.
- **e.** Change the time to one hour later using the Date and Time icon in the Control Panel.
- **f.** Return the settings to the original time and format, then close all open windows.

► Independent Challenge 3

Calculator is a Windows accessory that you can use to perform calculations.

- **a.** Start the Calculator, click Help on the menu bar, then click Help Topics.
- **b.** Click the Calculator book in the left pane, click Perform a simple calculation to view that help topic, then print it if you have a printer connected.
- **c.** Open the Perform a scientific calculation topic, then view the definition of a number system.
- **d.** Determine how many months you have to work to earn an additional week of vacation if you work for a company that provides one additional day of paid vacation for every 560 hours you work. (*Hint:* Divide 560 by the number of hours you work per month.)
- **e.** Close all open windows.

► Independent Challenge 4

You can customize many Windows features, including the appearance of the taskbar on the desktop.

- **a.** Right-click the taskbar, then click Lock the Taskbar to uncheck the command, if necessary.
- **b.** Position the pointer over the top border of the taskbar. When the pointer changes shape, drag up an inch.
- **c.** Resize the taskbar back to its original size.
- **d.** Right-click the Start button, then click Properties. Click the Taskbar tab.
- **e.** Click the Help button (a question mark), then click each check box to view the pop-up window describing it.
- **f.** Click the Start Menu tab, then click the Classic Start menu option button and view the change in the preview. (*Note:* Do not click OK.) Click Cancel.

▶ Visual Workshop

Use the skills you have learned in this unit to customize your desktop so it looks like the one in Figure A-18. Make sure you include the following:

- Calculator program minimized
- Vertical scroll bar in Control Panel window
- Large icons view in Control Panel window
- Rearranged icons on desktop; your icons may be different. (*Hint*: If the icons snap back to where they were, they are set to be automatically arranged. Right-click a blank area of the desktop, point to Arrange Icons By, then click Auto Arrange to deselect this option.)

Use the Print Screen key to make a copy of the screen, then print it from the Paint program. (To print from the Paint program, click the Start button on the taskbar, point to All Programs, point to Accessories, then click Paint; in the Paint program window, click Edit on the menu bar, then click Paste; click Yes to fit the image on the bitmap, click the Print button on the toolbar, then click Print in the Print dialog box. See your instructor or technical support person for assistance.)

When you have completed this exercise, be sure to return your settings and desktop back to their original arrangement.

FIGURE A-18

Working

with Programs, Files, and Folders

Objectives

- ► Create and save a WordPad document
- ► Open, edit, and save an existing Paint file
- ► Work with multiple programs
- ► Understand file management
- ► View files and create folders with My Computer
- ► Move and copy files with My Computer
- ► Manage files with Windows Explorer
- ► Search for files
- ► Delete and restore files

Most of your work on a computer involves using programs to create files. For example, you might use WordPad to create a resumé or Microsoft Excel to create a budget. The resumé and the budget are examples of **files**, electronic collections of data that you create and save on a disk. ◤ In this unit, you learn how to work with files and the programs you use to create them. You create new files, open and edit an existing file, and use the Clipboard to copy and paste data from one file to another. You also explore the file management features of Windows XP, using My Computer and Windows Explorer. Finally, you learn how to work more efficiently by managing files directly on your desktop.

Creating and Saving a WordPad Document

As with most programs, when you start WordPad, a new, blank document opens. To create a new file, such as a memo, you simply begin typing. Your work is automatically stored in your computer's random access memory (RAM) until you turn off your computer, at which point anything stored in the computer's RAM is erased. To store your work permanently, you must save your work as a file on a disk. You can save files either on an internal **hard disk**, which is built into your computer, usually the C: drive, or on a removable 3½" **floppy disk**, which you insert into a drive on your computer, usually the A: or B: drive, or on a **CD-ROM** or **Zip disk**, two other kinds of removable storage devices. (Before you can save a file on a floppy disk, the disk must be formatted; see the Appendix, "Formatting a Floppy Disk.") When you name a file, you can use up to 255 characters, including spaces and punctuation, using either upper- or lowercase letters. In this lesson, you start WordPad and create a file that contains the text shown in Figure B-1 and save the file to the drive and folder where your Project Files are stored.

1. Click the **Start button** on the taskbar, point to **All Programs**, point to **Accessories**, click **WordPad**, then click the **Maximize** button ▣ if the window does not fill your screen
   The WordPad program window opens. The blinking insertion point indicates where the text you type will appear.

2. Type **Memo**, then press [**Enter**] to move the insertion point to the next line

3. Press [**Enter**] again, then type the remaining text shown in Figure B-1, pressing [**Enter**] at the end of each line

4. Click **File** on the menu bar, then click **Save As**
   The Save As dialog box opens, as shown in Figure B-2. In this dialog box, you specify where you want your file saved and give your document a name.

5. Click the **Save in list arrow**, then click 3½ **Floppy (A:)**, or whichever drive contains your Project Files
   The drive containing your Project Files is now active, meaning that the contents of the drive appear in the Save in dialog box and that the file will now be saved in this drive.

6. Click in the **File name text box**, type **Memo**, then click the **Save button**
   Your memo is now saved as a WordPad file with the name "Memo" on your Project Disk. The WordPad title bar contains the name of the file. Now you can **format** the text, which changes its appearance to make it more readable or attractive.

7. Click to the left of the word **Memo**, drag the mouse to the right to highlight the word, then release the mouse button
   Now the text is highlighted, indicating that it is **selected**. This means that any action you make will be performed on the highlighted text.

8. Click the **Center button** ▤ on the Formatting toolbar, then click the **Bold button** Ⓑ on the Formatting toolbar
   The text is centered and bold.

9. Click the **Font Size list arrow** ⏷, click **16** in the list, then click the **Save button** ▣
   A **font** is a set of letters and numbers sharing a particular shape of type. The **font size** is measured in points; one **point** is ½ of an inch in height.

FIGURE B-1: Text to enter in WordPad

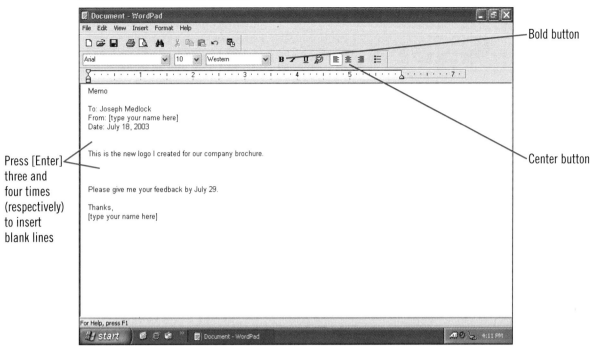

Bold button

Center button

Press [Enter] three and four times (respectively) to insert blank lines

FIGURE B-2: Save As dialog box

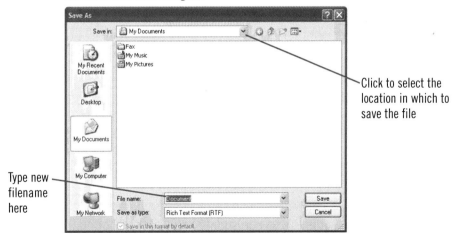

Click to select the location in which to save the file

Type new filename here

Opening, Editing, and Saving an Existing Paint File

Sometimes you create files from scratch, as you did in the previous lesson, but often you may want to work with a file you or someone else has already created. To do so, you need to open the file. Once you open a file, you can **edit** it, or make changes to it, such as adding or deleting text or changing the formatting. After editing a file, you can save it with the same filename, which means that you no longer will have the file in its original form, or you can save it with a different filename, so that the original file remains unchanged. ◄══════ In this lesson, you use Paint (a graphics program that comes with Windows XP) to open a file, edit it by changing a color, and then save the file with a new filename to leave the original file unchanged.

1. Click the **Start button** on the taskbar, point to **All Programs**, point to **Accessories**, click **Paint**, then click the **Maximize button** ▣ if the window doesn't fill the screen
The Paint program opens with a blank work area. If you wanted to create a file from scratch, you would begin working now. However, you want to open an existing file, located on your Project Disk.

2. Click **File** on the menu bar, then click **Open**
The Open dialog box works similarly to the Save As dialog box that you used in the previous lesson.

3. Click the **Look in list arrow**, then click **3½ Floppy (A:)**
The Paint files on your Project Disk are listed in the Open dialog box, as shown in Figure B-3.

QuickTip
You can also open a file by double-clicking it in the Open dialog box.

4. Click **Win B-1** in the list of files, and then click the **Open button**
The Open dialog box closes and the file named Win B-1 opens. Before you change this file, you should save it with a new filename, so that the original file is unchanged.

5. Click **File** on the menu bar, then click **Save As**

6. Make sure **3½ Floppy (A:)** appears in the Save in text box, select the text **Win B-1** in the File name text box, type **Logo**, click the **Save as type list arrow**, click **256 Color Bitmap**, then click the **Save button**
The Logo file appears in the Paint window, as shown in Figure B-4. Because you saved the file with a new name, you can edit it without changing the original file. You saved the file as a 256 Color Bitmap to conserve space on your floppy disk. You will now modify the logo by using buttons in the **Tool Box**, a toolbar of drawing tools, and the **Color Box**, a palette of colors from which you can choose.

7. Click the **Fill With Color button** 🖱 in the Tool Box, then click the **Light blue color box**, which is the fourth from the right in the bottom row
Notice how clicking a button in the Tool Box changes the mouse pointer. Now when you click an area in the image, it will be filled with the color you selected in the Color Box. See Table B-1 for a description of the tools in the Tool Box.

8. Move the pointer into the white area that represents the sky until the pointer changes to 🖱, then click
The sky is now blue.

9. Click **File** on the menu bar, then click **Save**
The change you made is saved to disk, using the same Logo filename.

FIGURE B-3: Open dialog box

List of files —

FIGURE B-4: Paint file saved with new filename

Name of file appears in title bar

Tool Box

Color Box

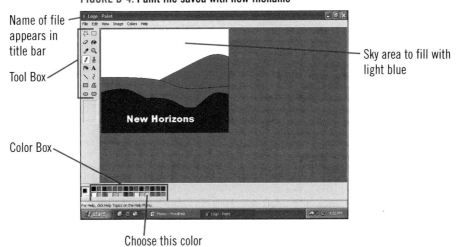

Sky area to fill with light blue

Choose this color

TABLE B-1: Paint Tool Box buttons

tool	description
Free-Form Select button	Selects a free-form section of the picture to move, copy, or edit
Select button	Selects a rectangular section of the picture to move, copy, or edit
Eraser button	Erases a portion of the picture using the selected eraser size and foreground color
Fill With Color button	Fills a closed shape or area with the current drawing color
Pick Color button	Picks up a color from the picture to use for drawing
Magnifier button	Changes the magnification; lists magnifications under the toolbar
Pencil button	Draws a free-form line one pixel wide
Ellipse button	Draws an ellipse with the selected fill style; hold down [Shift] to draw a circle
Brush button	Draws using a brush with the selected shape and size
Airbrush button	Produces a circular spray of dots
Text button	Inserts text into the picture
Line button	Draws a straight line with the selected width and foreground color
Curve button	Draws a wavy line with the selected width and foreground color
Rectangle button	Draws a rectangle with the selected fill style; hold down [Shift] to draw a square
Polygon button	Draws polygons from connected straight-line segments
Rounded Rectangle button	Draws rectangles with rounded corners using the selected fill style; hold down [Shift] to draw a rounded square

Windows XP

Working with Multiple Programs

A powerful feature of Windows is its capability to run more than one program at a time. For example, you might be working with a document in WordPad and want to search the Internet to find the answer to a question. You can start your **browser**, a program designed to access information on the Internet, without closing WordPad. When you find the information, you can leave your browser open and switch back to WordPad. Each open program is represented by a program button on the taskbar that you click to switch between programs. You can also copy data from one file to another (whether or not the files were created with the same Windows program) using the Clipboard, an area of memory on your computer's hard drive, and the Cut, Copy, and Paste commands. See Table B-2 for a description of these commands. ▚▬▬ In this lesson, you copy the logo graphic you worked with in the previous lesson into the memo you created in WordPad.

1. Click **Edit** on the menu bar, then click **Select All** to select the entire picture
   A dotted rectangle surrounds the picture, indicating it is selected, as shown in Figure B-5.

2. Click **Edit** on the menu bar, then click **Copy**
   The logo is copied to the Clipboard. When you **copy** an object onto the Clipboard, the object remains in its original location and is also available to be pasted into another location.

QuickTip

To switch between programs using the keyboard, press and hold down [Alt], press [Tab] until you select the program you want, then release [Alt].

3. Click the **WordPad program button** on the taskbar
   WordPad becomes the active program.

4. Click in the first line below the line that ends "for our company brochure."
   The insertion point indicates where the logo will be pasted.

5. Click the **Paste button** 📋 on the WordPad toolbar
   The contents of the Clipboard, in this case the logo, are pasted into the WordPad file, as shown in Figure B-6.

6. Click the WordPad **Close button**; click **Yes** to save changes
   Your WordPad document and the WordPad program close. Paint is now the active program.

7. Click the Paint **Close button**; if you are prompted to save changes, click **Yes**
   Your Paint document and the Paint program close. You return to the desktop.

CLUES TO USE

Other Programs that Come with Windows XP

WordPad and Paint are just two of many programs that come with Windows XP. From the All Programs menu on the Start menu, you can access everything from games and entertainment programs to powerful communications software and disk maintenance programs without installing anything other than Windows XP. For example, from the Accessories menu, you can open a simple calculator; start Windows Movie Maker to create, edit, and share movie files; and use the Address Book to keep track of your contacts. From the Communications submenu, you can use NetMeeting to set up a voice and/or video conference over the Internet, or use the Remote Desktop Connection to allow another person to access your computer for diagnosing and solving computer problems. Several other menus and submenus display programs and tools that come with Windows XP. You can get a brief description of each by holding your mouse pointer over the name of the program in the menu. You might have to install some of these programs from the Windows CD if they don't appear on the menus.

FIGURE B-5: Selecting the logo to copy and paste into the Memo file

Dotted line indicates selected area

FIGURE B-6: Memo with pasted logo

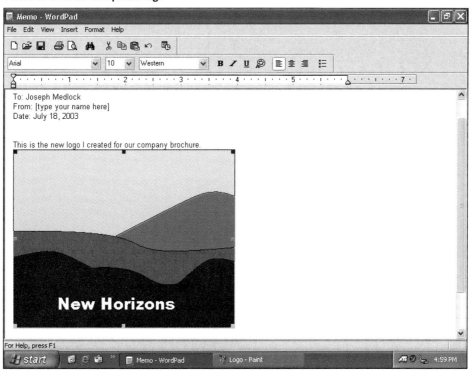

TABLE B-2: Overview of cutting, copying, and pasting

toolbar button	function	keyboard shortcut
Cut	Removes selected information from a file and places it on the Clipboard	[Ctrl][X]
Copy	Places a copy of the selected information on the Clipboard, leaving the file intact	[Ctrl][C]
Paste	Inserts whatever is currently on the Clipboard into another location within the same file or into another file (depending on where you place the insertion point)	[Ctrl][V]

Windows XP

Understanding File Management

After you have created and saved numerous files, the process of organizing and keeping track of all of your files (referred to as **file management**) can be a challenge. Fortunately, Windows provides tools to keep everything organized so you can easily locate the files you need, move files to new locations, and delete files you no longer need. There are two main tools for managing your files: My Computer and Windows Explorer. In this lesson, you preview the ways you can use My Computer and Windows Explorer to manage your files.

Windows XP gives you the ability to:

▶ **Create folders in which you can save and organize your files**
Folders are areas on a floppy disk (or other removable storage medium) or hard disk that help you organize your files, just as folders in a filing cabinet help you store and organize your papers. For example, you might create a folder for your work documents and another folder for your personal files. Folders can also contain other folders, which creates a more complex structure of folders and files, called a **file hierarchy**. See Figure B-7 for an example of how files can be organized.

▶ **Examine and organize the hierarchy of files and folders**
You can use either My Computer or Windows Explorer to see and manipulate the overall structure of your files and folders. By examining your file hierarchy with these tools, you can better organize the contents of your computer and adjust the hierarchy to meet your needs. Figures B-8 and B-9 illustrate how My Computer and Windows Explorer list folders and files.

▶ **Copy, move, and rename files and folders**
If you decide that a file belongs in a different folder, you can move it to another folder. You can also rename a file if you decide a different name is more descriptive. If you want to keep a copy of a file in more than one folder, you can copy it to new folders.

▶ **Delete files and folders you no longer need and restore files you delete accidentally**
Deleting files and folders you are sure you don't need frees up disk space and keeps your file hierarchy more organized. The **Recycle Bin**, a space on your computer's hard disk that stores deleted files, allows you to restore files you deleted by accident. To free up disk space, you should occasionally check to make sure you don't need the contents of the Recycle Bin and then delete the files permanently from your hard drive.

▶ **Locate files quickly with the Windows XP Search feature**
As you create more files and folders, you may forget where you placed a certain file or you may forget what name you used when you saved a file. With Search, you can locate files by providing only partial names or other facts you know about the file, such as the file type (for example, a WordPad document or a Paint graphic) or the date the file was created or modified.

▶ **Use shortcuts**
If a file or folder you use often is located several levels down in your file hierarchy (in a folder within a folder, within a folder), it might take you several steps to access it. To save time accessing the files and programs you use frequently, you can create shortcuts to them. A **shortcut** is a link that gives you quick access to a particular file, folder, or program.

QuickTip

To browse My Computer using multiple windows, click Tools on the menu bar, and then click Folder Options. In the Folder Options dialog box, click the General tab, and then under Browse Folders, click the Open each folder in its own window option button. Each time you open a new folder, a new window opens, leaving the previous folder's window open so that you can view both at the same time.

FIGURE B-7: Sample file hierarchy

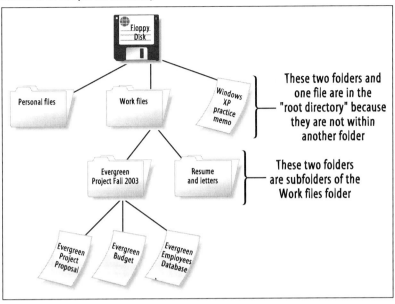

These two folders and one file are in the "root directory" because they are not within another folder

These two folders are subfolders of the Work files folder

FIGURE B-8: Evergreen Project folder shown in My Computer

Tasks related to selected object appear here

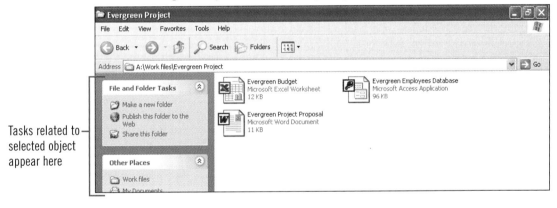

FIGURE B-9: Evergreen Project folder shown in Windows Explorer

File hierarchy is visible; the selected folder's contents appear in the right pane

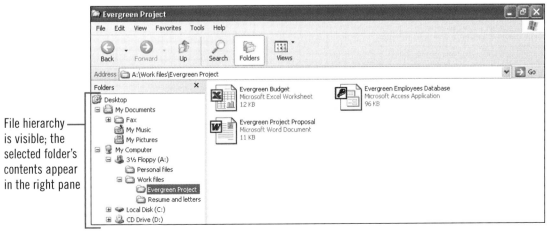

Windows XP

Viewing Files and Creating Folders with My Computer

My Computer shows the contents of your computer, including files, folders, programs, disk drives, and printers. You can click the icons to view that object's contents or properties. You use the My Computer Explorer Bar, menu bar, and toolbar to manage your files. See Table B-3 for a description of the toolbar buttons. ⬤━━ In this lesson, you use My Computer to look at your computer's file hierarchy, then you create two new folders on your Project Disk.

Steps123⁴

Trouble?

If you do not see the My Computer icon on your desktop, click the Start button, and then click My Computer. If you do not see the toolbar, click View on the menu bar, point to Toolbars, and then click Standard Buttons. If you do not see the Address bar, click View, point to Toolbar, and then click Address Bar.

Trouble?

If you are in a lab setting, you may not have access to the My Documents folder. See your instructor or technical support person for assistance.

QuickTip

You can click the list arrow next to the Back or Forward buttons to quickly view locations you've viewed recently.

QuickTip

You can also rename a folder or file by pressing [F2], typing the new name, then pressing [Enter].

1. Double-click the **My Computer icon** 🖳 on your desktop, then click the **Maximize button** ☐ if the My Computer window does not fill the screen
   My Computer displays the contents of your computer, as shown in Figure B-10. The left pane, called the **Explorer Bar**, displays tasks related to whatever is selected in the right pane.

2. Make sure your Project Disk is in the floppy disk drive, then double-click the **3½ Floppy (A:) icon**
   The contents of your Project Disk appear in the window. Each file is represented by an icon, which varies in appearance depending on the program that was used to create the file. If Microsoft Word is installed on your computer, the Word icon appears for the WordPad files; if not, the WordPad icon appears.

3. Click the **Address list arrow** on the Address bar, as shown in Figure B-10, then click **My Documents**
   The window changes to show the contents of the My Documents folder on your computer's hard drive. The Address bar allows you to open and view a drive, folder, or even a Web page. You can also type in the Address bar to go to a different drive, folder, or Web page. For example, typing "C:\" will display the contents of your C: drive, and typing "http://www.microsoft.com" opens Microsoft's Web site if your computer is connected to the Internet.

4. Click the **Back button** ◁ on the Standard Buttons toolbar
   The Back button displays the previous location, in this case, your Project Disk.

5. Click the **Views button list arrow** ▦ ▾ on the Standard Buttons toolbar, then click **Details**
   Details view shows not only the files and folders, but also the sizes of the files, the types of files, folders, or drives and the date the files were last modified.

6. In the File and Folder Tasks pane, click **Make a new folder**
   A new folder called "New Folder" is created on your Project Disk, as shown in Figure B-11. You can also create a new folder by right-clicking in the blank area of the My Computer window, clicking New, then clicking Folder.

7. If necessary, click to select the folder, then click **Rename this folder** in the File and Folder Tasks pane; type **Windows XP Practice**, then press **[Enter]**
   Choosing descriptive names for your folders helps you remember their contents.

8. Double-click the **Windows XP Practice folder**, repeat Steps 6 and 7 to create a new folder in the Windows XP Practice folder, name the folder **Brochure**, then press **[Enter]**

9. Click the **Up button** 🗁 to return to the root directory of your Project Disk

FIGURE B-10: **My Computer window**

Menu bar

Address bar

Standard Buttons toolbar

Address list arrow

Your icons may differ

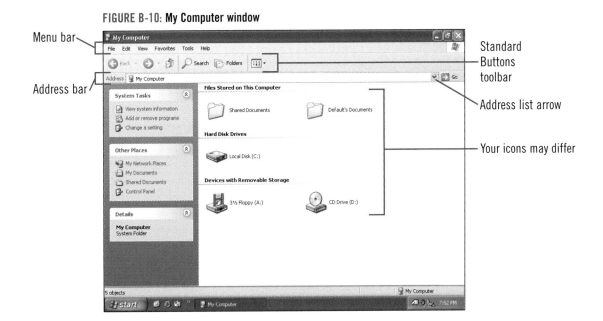

FIGURE B-11: **Creating a new folder**

Back button

Folder is located on the A: drive

You'll rename the new folder; yours might appear selected

TABLE B-3: **Buttons on the Standard Buttons toolbar in My Computer**

button	function
Back button	Moves back one location in the list of locations you have recently viewed
Forward button	Moves forward one location in the list of locations you have recently viewed
Up button	Moves up one level in the file hierarchy
Search button	Opens the Search Companion task pane, where you can choose from various options to search for files, computers, Web pages, or people on the Internet
Folders button	Opens the Folders task pane, where you can easily view and manage your computer's file hierarchy
Views button	Lists the contents of My Computer using different views

Moving and Copying Files with My Computer

You can move a file or folder from one location to another using a variety of methods in My Computer. If the file or folder and the location to which you want to move it are both visible, you can simply drag the item from one location to another. You can also use the Cut, Copy, and Paste commands on the Edit menu, or right-click a file or folder and click the appropriate option on the menu that appears. Perhaps the most powerful file management tool in My Computer is the Common Tasks pane. When you select any item in My Computer, the Common Tasks pane changes to the File and Folder Tasks pane, listing tasks you can typically perform with the selected item. For example, if you select a file, the options in the Files and Folders task pane include "Rename this file," "Move this file," and "Delete this file," among many others. If you select a folder, file management tasks for folders appear. If you select more than one object, tasks appear that relate to manipulating multiple objects. You can also right-click any file or folder and choose the Send To command to "send" it to another location – most often a floppy disk or other removable storage medium. This **backs up** the files, making copies of them in case you have computer trouble (which can cause you to lose files from your hard disk). In this lesson, you move your files into the folder you created in the last lesson.

Steps

1. Click the **Win B-1 file**, hold down the mouse button and drag the file onto the **Windows XP Practice folder**, as shown in Figure B-12, then release the mouse button
   Win B-1 is moved into the Windows XP Practice folder.

2. Double-click the **Windows XP Practice folder** and confirm that the folder contains the Win B-1 file as well as the Brochure folder

QuickTip
It is easy to confuse the Back button with the Up button. The Back button returns you to the last location you viewed, no matter where it is in your folder hierarchy. The Up button displays the next level up in the folder hierarchy, no matter what you last viewed.

3. Click the **Up button** 🖫 on the Standard Buttons toolbar, as shown in Figure B-12
   You return to the root directory of your Project Disk. The Up button shows the next level up in the folder hierarchy.

4. Click the **Logo file**, press and hold down **[Shift]**, then click the **Memo file**
   Both files are selected. Table B-4 describes methods for selecting multiple objects.

5. Click **Move the selected items** in the File and Folder Tasks pane
   The filenames turn gray, and the Move Items dialog box opens, as shown in Figure B-13.

6. Click the plus sign ⊞ next to My Computer if you do not see 3½ Floppy (A:) listed, click the **3½ Floppy (A:)** drive, click the **Windows XP Practice folder**, click the **Brochure folder**, then click **Move**
   The two files are moved to the Brochure folder. Only the Windows XP Practice folder and the Win B-2 file remain in the root directory.

7. Click the **Close button** in the 3½ Floppy (A:) (My Computer) window

FIGURE B-12: Dragging a file from one folder to another

Up button

Common Tasks pane

When you drag a file to a new location, the file and location are highlighted, indicating that both are being used

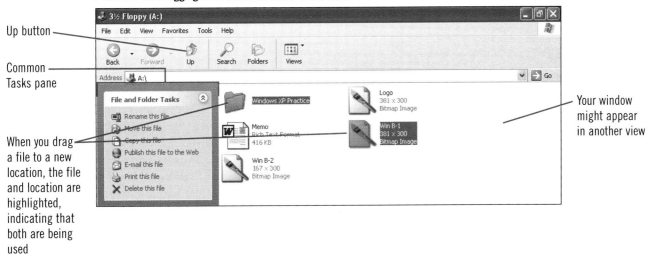

Your window might appear in another view

FIGURE B-13: Moving files

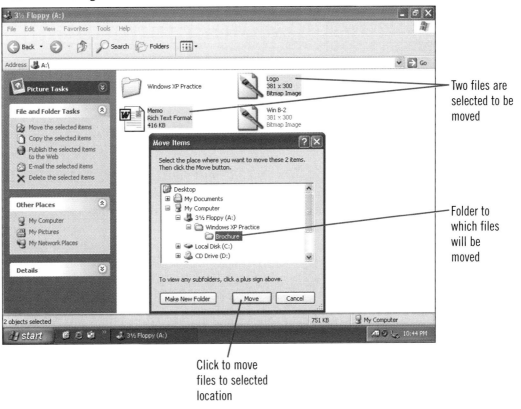

Two files are selected to be moved

Folder to which files will be moved

Click to move files to selected location

TABLE B-4: Techniques for selecting multiple files and folders

to select	do this
Individual objects not grouped together	Click the first object you want to select, then press and hold down [Ctrl] as you click each additional object you want to add to the selection
Objects grouped together	Click the first object you want to select, then press and hold down [Shift] as you click the last object in the list of objects you want to select; all the objects listed between the first and last objects are selected

Windows XP

Managing Files with Windows Explorer

As with My Computer, you can use Windows Explorer to copy, move, delete, and rename files and folders. However, in their default settings, My Computer and Windows Explorer look a little different and work in slightly different ways. In My Computer, the Explorer Bar displays the File and Folder Tasks pane when you select files or folders. In Windows Explorer, the Explorer Bar displays the Folders pane, which allows you to see and manipulate the overall structure of the contents of your computer or network while you work with individual files and folders within that structure. This allows you to work with more than one computer, folder, or file at once. Note that you can change the view in My Computer to show the Folders pane, and in Windows Explorer to view the File and Folder Tasks pane. In this lesson, you copy a folder from your Project Disk into the My Documents folder on your hard disk and then rename the folder.

Steps

Trouble?

If you do not see the toolbar, click View on the menu bar, point to Toolbars, then click Standard Buttons. If you do not see the Address bar, click View, point to Toolbars, then click Address Bar.

1. Click the **Start button**, point to **All Programs**, point to **Accessories**, click **Windows Explorer**, then maximize the window if necessary

Windows Explorer opens, as shown in Figure B-14. The Folders pane on the left displays the drives and folders on your computer in a hierarchy. The right pane displays the contents of whatever drive or folder is currently selected in the Folders pane. Each pane has its own set of scroll bars, so that scrolling in one pane won't affect the other.

2. Click **View** on the menu bar, then click **Details** if it is not already selected

Remember that a bullet point or check mark next to a command on the menu indicates that it's selected.

Trouble?

If you cannot see the A: drive, you may have to click the plus sign (+) next to My Computer to view the available drives on your computer.

3. In the Folders pane, scroll to and click **3½ Floppy (A:)**

The contents of your Project Disk appear in the right pane.

4. In the Folders pane, click the **plus sign (+)** next to 3½ Floppy (A:), if necessary

You click the plus sign (+) or minus sign (-) next to any item in the left pane to show or hide the different levels of the file hierarchy, so that you don't always have to look at the entire structure of your computer or network. A plus sign (+) next to an item indicates there are additional folders within that object. A minus sign (-) indicates the next level of the hierarchy is shown. Clicking the + displays (or "expands") the next level; clicking the – hides (or "collapses") it. When neither a + nor a – appears next to an icon, it means that the object does not have any folders in it, although it may have files.

5. In the Folders pane, click the **Windows XP Practice folder**

The contents of the Windows XP Practice folder appear in the right pane, as shown in Figure B-15. Double-clicking an item in the Folders pane that has a + next to it displays its contents in the right pane and also expands the next level in the Folders pane.

Trouble?

If you are working in a lab setting, you may not be able to add items to your My Documents folder. Skip, but read carefully, Steps 6, 7, and 8 if you are unable to complete them.

6. In the Folders pane, drag the **Windows XP Practice folder** on top of the **My Documents folder**, then release the mouse button

When you drag files or folders from one drive to a different drive, they are copied rather than moved.

7. In the Folders pane, click the **My Documents folder**

The Windows XP Practice folder should now appear in the list of folders in the right pane. You may have to scroll to see it. Now you should rename the folder so you can distinguish the original folder from the copy.

8. Right-click the **Windows XP Practice folder** in the right pane, click **Rename** in the shortcut menu, type **Windows XP Copy**, then press [Enter]

FIGURE B-14: Windows Explorer window

Left pane,
known as the
Folders list
or the
Explorer Bar

Your list of
devices,
folders, and
files will
differ

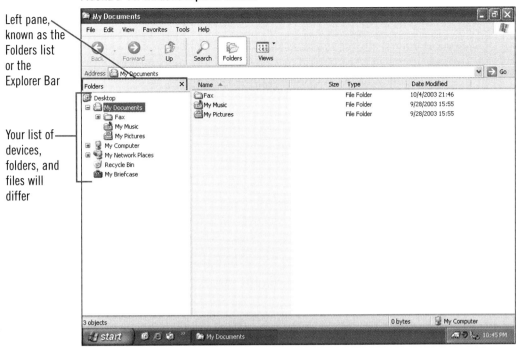

FIGURE B-15: Contents of Windows XP Practice folder

Windows XP
Practice folder
selected in
left pane

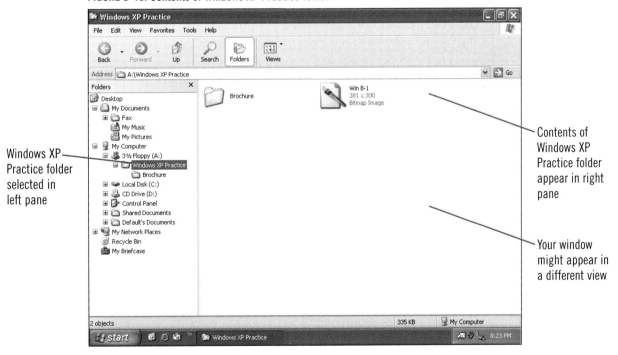

Contents of
Windows XP
Practice folder
appear in right
pane

Your window
might appear in
a different view

Searching for Files

After you've worked a while on your computer, saving, deleting, and modifying files and folders, you may forget where you've saved an item or what you named it. Or, you may want to send an e-mail to someone, but you can't remember how the name is spelled. You can use the **Windows XP Search** feature to quickly find any kind of object, from a Word document or a movie file to a computer on your network or a person in your address book. If you're connected to the Internet, you can use Search to locate Web pages and people on the Internet. In this lesson, you search for a file on your Project Disk.

Steps

QuickTip

You can also start the Search Companion by clicking the Start button and then clicking Search. To change the way the Search tool works (such as whether the animated dog appears), click Change preferences at the bottom of the Search Companion pane.

1. Click the **Search button** 🔎 on the Standard Buttons toolbar
   The Explorer Bar changes to display the Search Companion pane, as shown in Figure B-16. Let's assume you can't remember where you placed the Logo file you created earlier. You know that it is a picture file and that it is somewhere on your floppy disk.

2. In the Search Companion pane, click **Pictures, music, or video**; in the list that appears, click the **Pictures and Photos check box**, then type **Logo** in the All or part of the file name text box, as shown in Figure B-17

3. Click **Use advanced search options** to open a larger pane, click the **Look in list arrow**, click **3½ Floppy (A:)**, then click the **Search button** at the bottom of the Search Companion pane
   The search results are displayed in the right pane and options for further searching are displayed in the Search Companion pane.

4. Click the **Logo icon** in the right pane, click **File** on the menu bar, point to **Open With**, and then click **Paint**

Trouble?

If you don't like the way your clouds look, click Edit on the menu bar, click Undo, then repeat Step 5.

5. Click the **Airbrush tool** ✍, click the **white color box** in the Color box (the first one in the second row), then drag or click in the sky to make clouds

6. Save the file without changing the name and close Paint

Accessing files, folders, programs, and drives you use often

As you continue to use your computer, you will probably find that you use certain files, folders, programs, and disk drives almost every day. You can create a shortcut, an icon that represents an object stored somewhere else, and place it on the desktop. From the desktop, you double-click the shortcut to open the item, whether it's a file, folder, program, or disk drive. To create a shortcut on the desktop, view the object in My Computer or Windows Explorer, size the window so you can see both the object and part of the desktop at the same time, use the *right* mouse button to drag the object to the desktop, and then click Create Shortcuts Here. To delete the shortcut, select it and press [Delete]. The original file, folder, or program will not be affected. To pin a program to the Start menu, which places it conveniently at the top of the left side of the menu, open the Start menu as far as needed to view the program you want to pin, right-click the program name, and then click Pin to Start menu. To remove it, right-click it in its new position and then click Unpin from Start menu.

FIGURE B-16: Getting ready to search

Search button

Search Companion pane

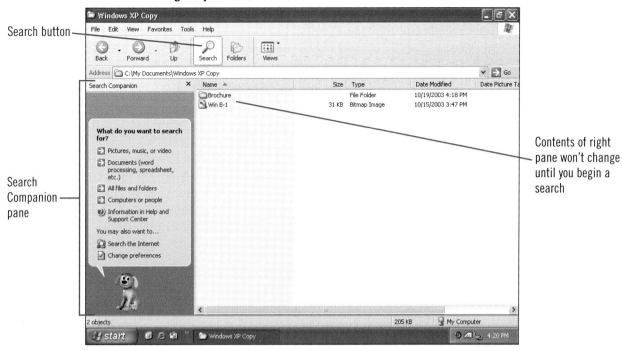

Contents of right pane won't change until you begin a search

FIGURE B-17: Specifying search options

Select this check box

Enter search text here

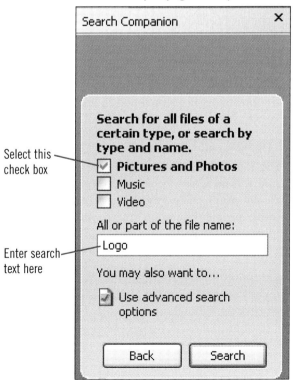

Deleting and Restoring Files

To save disk space and manage your files more effectively, you should **delete** (or remove) files you no longer need. There are many ways to delete files and folders from the My Computer and Windows Explorer windows, as well as from the Windows XP desktop. Because files deleted from your hard disk are stored in the Recycle Bin until you remove them permanently by emptying the Recycle Bin, you can restore any files you might have deleted accidentally. However, note that when you delete files from your floppy disk, they are not stored in the Recycle Bin – they are permanently deleted. See Table B-5 for an overview of deleting and restoring files. In this lesson, you delete a file by dragging it to the Recycle Bin, you restore it, and then you delete a folder by using the Delete command in Windows Explorer.

1. Click the **Folders button** 📂, then click the **Restore button** 🗗 on the Search Results (Windows Explorer) title bar
   You should be able to see the Recycle Bin icon on your desktop, as shown in Figure B-18. If you can't see the Recycle Bin, resize or move the Windows Explorer window until it is visible.

2. If necessary, select the **Windows XP Copy folder** in the left pane of Windows Explorer

3. Drag the **Windows XP Copy folder** from the left pane to the **Recycle Bin** on the desktop, as shown in Figure B-18, then click **Yes** to confirm the deletion, if necessary
   The folder no longer appears in Windows Explorer because you have moved it to the Recycle Bin.

4. Double-click the **Recycle Bin icon** on the desktop, then scroll if necessary until you can see the **Windows XP Copy folder**
   The Recycle Bin window opens, as shown in Figure B-19. Depending on the number of files already deleted on your computer, your window might look different.

5. Click the **Windows XP Copy folder**, then click **Restore this item** in the Recycle Bin Tasks pane
   The Windows XP Copy folder is restored and should now appear in the Windows Explorer window.

6. Right-click the **Windows XP Copy folder** in the right pane of Windows Explorer, click **Delete** on the shortcut menu, then click **Yes**
   When you are sure you no longer need files you've moved into the Recycle Bin, you can empty the Recycle Bin. You won't do this now, in case you are working on a computer that you share with other people. But when you're working on your own machine, open the Recycle Bin window, verify that you don't need any of the files or folders in it, then click Empty the Recycle Bin in the Recycle Bin Tasks pane.

7. Close the Recycle Bin and Windows Explorer
   If you minimized the Recycle Bin in Step 5, click its program button to open the Recycle Bin window, and then click the Close button.

FIGURE B-18: Dragging a folder to delete it

Your desktop
background and
icons might differ

Drag the folder here

Folder located
in the My
Documents
folder

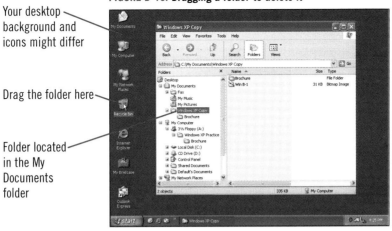

FIGURE B-19: Recycle Bin window

Deleted folder

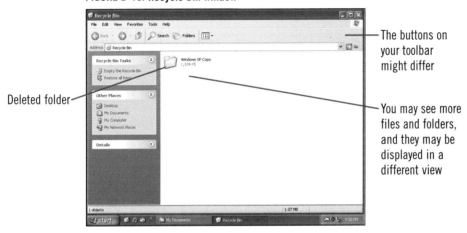

The buttons on
your toolbar
might differ

You may see more
files and folders,
and they may be
displayed in a
different view

TABLE B-5: Methods for deleting and restoring files

ways to delete a file	ways to restore a file from the Recycle Bin
If File and Folder Tasks pane is open, click the file, then click Delete this file	Click Edit, then click Undo Delete
Select the file, then press [Delete]	Select the file in the Recycle Bin window, then click Restore this file
Right-click the file, then click Delete on the shortcut menu	Right-click the file in the Recycle Bin window, then click Restore
Drag the file to the Recycle Bin	Drag the file from the Recycle Bin to any other location

Customizing your Recycle Bin

You can set your Recycle Bin according to how you like to delete and restore files. For example, if you do not want files to go to the Recycle Bin but rather want them to be immediately and permanently deleted, right-click the Recycle Bin, click Properties, then click the Do Not Move Files to the Recycle Bin check box. If you find that the Recycle Bin fills up too fast and you are not ready to delete the files permanently, you can increase the amount of disk space devoted to the Recycle Bin by moving the Maximum Size of Recycle Bin slider to the right. This, of course, reduces the amount of disk space you have available for other things. Also, you can choose not to have the Confirm File Delete dialog box open when you send files to the Recycle Bin. See your instructor or technical support person before changing any of the Recycle Bin settings.

Practice

► Concepts Review

Label each of the elements of the Windows Explorer window shown in Figure B-20.

FIGURE B-20

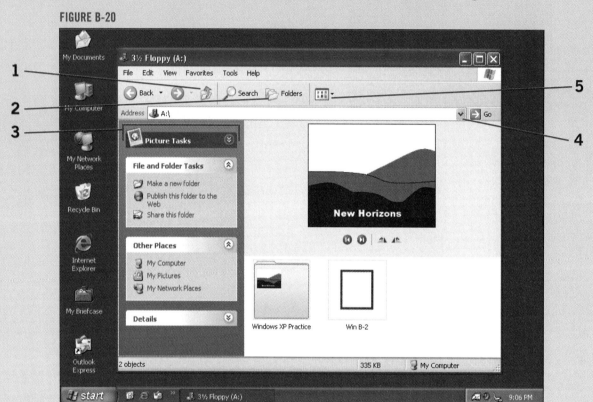

Match each of the statements with the term it describes.

6. Electronic collections of data
7. Your computer's temporary storage area
8. Temporary location of information you wish to paste into another location
9. Storage areas on your hard drive for files, folders, and programs
10. Structure of files and folders

a. RAM
b. Folders
c. Files
d. File hierarchy
e. Clipboard

Select the best answer from the list of choices.

11. To prepare a floppy disk to save your files, you must first make sure
   a. files are copied to the disk.
   b. the disk is formatted.
   c. all the files that might be on the disk are erased.
   d. the files are on the Clipboard.

12. You can use My Computer to
   a. create a drawing of your computer.
   b. view the contents of a folder.
   c. change the appearance of your desktop.
   d. add text to a WordPad file.

13. Which of the following best describes WordPad?
   a. A program for organizing files
   b. A program for performing financial analysis
   c. A program for creating basic text documents
   d. A program for creating graphics

14. **Which of the following is NOT a way to move a file from one folder to another?**
    a. Open the file and drag its program window to the new folder.
    b. In My Computer or Windows Explorer, drag the selected file to the new folder.
    c. Use the Move this file command in the File and Folder Tasks pane.
    d. Use the [Ctrl][X] and [Ctrl][V] keyboard shortcuts while in the My Computer or the Windows Explorer window.

15. **In which of the following can you, by default, view the hierarchy of drives, folders, and files in a split pane window?**
    a. Windows Explorer
    b. All Programs
    c. My Computer
    d. WordPad

16. **To restore files that you have sent to the Recycle Bin,**
    a. click File, then click Empty Recycle Bin.
    b. click Edit, then click Undo Delete.
    c. click File, then click Undo.
    d. You cannot retrieve files sent to the Recycle Bin.

17. **To select files that are not grouped together, select the first file, then**
    a. press [Shift] while selecting the second file.
    b. press [Alt] while selecting the second file.
    c. press [Ctrl] while selecting the second file.
    d. click the second file.

18. **Pressing [Backspace]**
    a. deletes the character to the right of the cursor.
    b. deletes the character to the left of the cursor.
    c. moves the insertion point one character to the right.
    d. deletes all text to the left of the cursor.

19. **The size of a font is measured in**
    a. centimeters.
    b. points.
    c. places.
    d. millimeters.

20. **The Back button on the My Computer toolbar**
    a. starts the last program you used.
    b. displays the next level of the file hierarchy.
    c. backs up the currently selected file.
    d. displays the last location you visited.

► Skills Review

1. **Create and save a WordPad file.**
   a. Start Windows, then start WordPad.
   b. Type **My Drawing Ability**, then press [Enter] three times.
   c. Save the document as **Drawing Ability** to your Project Disk, but do not close it.

2. **Open, edit, and save an existing Paint file.**
   a. Start Paint and open the file Win B-2 on your Project Disk.
   b. Save the picture with the filename **First Unique Art** as a 256-color bitmap file to your Project Disk.
   c. Inside the picture frame, use [Shift] with the Ellipse tool to create a circle, fill it with purple, switch to yellow, then use [Shift] with the Rectangle tool to place a square inside the circle. Fill the square with yellow.
   d. Save the file, but do not close it. (Click Yes, if necessary to replace the file.)

3. **Work with multiple programs.**
   a. Select the entire graphic and copy it to the Clipboard, then switch to WordPad.
   b. Place the insertion point in the last blank line, paste the graphic into your document, then deselect the graphic.
   c. Save the changes to your WordPad document. Switch to Paint.
   d. Using the Fill With Color tool, change the color of a filled area of your graphic.
   e. Save the revised graphic with the new name **Second Unique Art** as a 256-color bitmap on your Project Disk.
   f. Select the entire graphic and copy it to the Clipboard.
   g. Switch to WordPad, move the insertion point to the line below the graphic by clicking below the graphic and pressing [Enter], type **This is another version of my graphic:** below the first picture, then press [Enter].

h. Paste the second graphic under the text you just typed.

i. Save the changed WordPad document as **Two Drawing Examples** to your Project Disk. Close Paint and WordPad.

4. View files and create folders with My Computer.

  a. Open My Computer. Double-click the drive that contains your Project Disk.

  b. Create a new folder on your Project Disk by clicking File, pointing to New, then clicking Folder, and name the new folder **Review**.

  c. Open the folder to display its contents (it is empty).

  d. Use the Address bar to view the My Documents folder.

  e. Create a folder in the My Documents folder called **Temporary**, then use the Back button to view the Review folder.

  f. Create two new folders in the Review folder, one named **Documents** and the other named **Artwork**.

  g. Click the Forward button as many times as necessary to view the contents of the My Documents folder.

  h. Change the view to Details if necessary.

5. Move and copy files with My Computer.

  a. Use the Address bar to view your Project Disk. Switch to Details view, if necessary.

  b. Press the [Shift] key while selecting First Unique Art and Second Unique Art, then cut and paste them into the Artwork folder.

  c. Use the Back button to view the contents of Project Disk.

  d. Select the two WordPad files, Drawing Ability and Two Drawing Examples, then move them into the Review folder.

  e. Open the Review folder, select the two WordPad files again, move them into the Documents folder, then close My Computer.

6. Manage files with Windows Explorer.

  a. Open Windows Explorer and view the contents of the Artwork folder in the right pane.

  b. Select the two Paint files.

  c. Drag the two Paint files from the Artwork folder to the Temporary folder in the My Documents folder to copy – not move – them.

  d. View the contents of the Documents folder in the right pane, then select the two WordPad files.

  e. Repeat Step c to copy the files to the Temporary folder in the My Documents folder.

  f. View the contents of the Temporary folder in the right pane to verify that the four files are there.

7. Search for files.

  a. Open the Search companion from Windows Explorer.

  b. Search for the First Unique Art file on your Project Disk.

  c. Close the Search Results window.

8. Delete and restore files and folders.

  a. If necessary, open and resize the Windows Explorer window so you can see the Recycle Bin icon on the desktop, then scroll in Windows Explorer so you can see the Temporary folder in the left pane.

  b. Delete the Temporary folder from the My Documents folder by dragging it to the Recycle Bin.

  c. Click Yes to confirm the deletion, if necessary.

  d. Open the Recycle Bin, restore the Temporary folder and its files to your hard disk, and then close the Recycle Bin. (*Note:* If your Recycle Bin is empty, your computer is set to automatically delete items in the Recycle Bin.)

  e. Delete the Temporary folder again by clicking to select it and then pressing [Delete]. Click Yes to confirm the deletion.

▶ Independent Challenge 1

You have decided to start a bakery business and you want to use Windows XP to create and organize the files for the business.

  a. Create two new folders on your Project Disk, one named **Advertising** and one named **Customers**.

  b. Use WordPad to create a letter inviting new customers to the open house for the new bakery, then save it as **Open House Letter** in the Customers folder.

  c. Use WordPad to create a new document that lists five tasks that need to get done before the business opens (such as purchasing equipment, decorating the interior, and ordering supplies), then save it as **Business Plan** to your Project Disk, but don't place it in a folder.

  d. Use Paint to create a simple logo for the bakery, save it as a 256-color bitmap named **Bakery Logo**, then place it in the Advertising folder.

  e. Print the three files.

▶ Independent Challenge 2

To complete this Independent Challenge, you will need a second formatted, blank floppy disk. Write **IC2** on the disk label, then complete the steps below. Follow the guidelines listed here to create the file hierarchy shown in Figure B-21.

  a. In the My Documents folder on your hard drive, create one folder named IC2 and a second named Project Disk 1.

  b. Copy the contents of your first Project Disk into the new Project Disk 1 folder. This will give you access to your files as you complete these steps.

FIGURE B-21

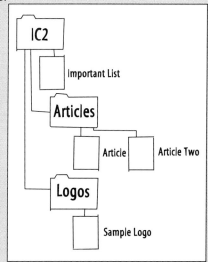

  c. Place your blank IC2 disk into the floppy drive.

  d. Start WordPad, then create a new file that contains a list of things to get done. Save the file as **To Do List** to your IC2 Disk.

  e. Start My Computer and copy the To Do List from your IC2 Disk to the IC2 folder and rename the file in the IC2 folder **Important List**.

  f. Copy the Open House Letter file from your Project Disk 1 folder to the IC2 folder. Rename the file **Article**.

  g. Copy the Memo file from your Project Disk 1 folder to the IC2 folder in the My Documents folder and rename it **Article Two**.

  h. Copy the Logo file from your Project Disk 1 folder to the IC2 folder and rename the file **Sample Logo**.

  i. Move the files into the folders shown in Figure B-21.

  j. Copy the IC2 folder to your IC2 Disk, then delete the Project Disk 1 and IC2 folders from the My Documents folder.

▶ Independent Challenge 3

With Windows XP, you can access the Web from My Computer and Windows Explorer, allowing you to search for information located not only on your computer or network but also on any computer on the Internet.

  a. Start Windows Explorer, then click in the Address bar so the current location is selected, type **www.microsoft.com**, then press [Enter].

  b. Connect to the Internet if necessary. The Microsoft Web page appears in the right pane of Windows Explorer.

c. Click in the Address bar, then type **www.course.com**, press [Enter], and then wait a moment while the Course Technology Web page opens.

d. Make sure your Project Disk is in the floppy disk drive, then click 3½ Floppy (A:) in the left pane.

e. Click the Back button list arrow, then click Microsoft's home page.

f. Capture a picture of your desktop by pressing [Print Screen] (usually located on the upper-right side of your keyboard). This stores the picture on the Clipboard. Open the Paint program, paste the contents of the Clipboard into the drawing window, clicking No if asked to enlarge the Bitmap, then print the picture.

g. Close Paint without saving your changes.

h. Close Windows Explorer, then disconnect from the Internet if necessary.

► Independent Challenge 4

Open Windows Explorer, make sure you can see the drive that contains your Project Disk listed in the left pane, use the right mouse button to drag the drive to a blank area on the desktop, then click Create Shortcuts Here. Then capture a picture of your desktop showing the new shortcut: press [Print Screen], located on the upper-right side of your keyboard. Then open the Paint program and paste the contents of the Clipboard into the drawing window. Print the screen, close Paint without saving your changes, then delete the shortcut when you are finished.

► Visual Workshop

Recreate the screen shown in Figure B-22, which shows the Search Results window with the Memo file listed, one shortcut on the desktop, and one open (but minimized) file. Press [Print Screen] to make a copy of the screen, (a copy of the screen is placed on the Clipboard), open Paint, click Paste to paste the screen picture into Paint, then print the Paint file. Close Paint without saving your changes, and then return your desktop to its original state. Your desktop might have different icons and a different background.

FIGURE B-22

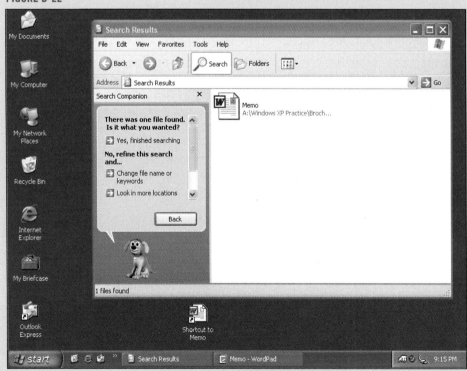

Formatting
a Floppy Disk

A **disk** is a device on which you can store electronic data. Disks
come in a variety of sizes and have varying storage capacities. Your
computer's **hard disk**, one of its internal devices, can store large
amounts of data. **Floppy disks**, on the other hand, are smaller,
inexpensive, and portable. Most floppy disks that you buy today are
3½-inch disks (the diameter of the inside, circular part of the disk) and
are already formatted. Check the package that your disk came in for the
word "formatted" or "pre-formatted;" such disks do not require further
formatting. If your package says "unformatted," then you should follow
the steps in this appendix.   In this appendix, you will prepare a
floppy disk for use.

Windows XP

Formatting a Floppy Disk

In order for an operating system to be able to store data on a disk, the disk must be formatted. **Formatting** prepares a disk so it can store information. Usually, floppy disks are formatted when you buy them, but if not, you can format them yourself using Windows XP. To complete the following steps, you need a blank floppy disk or a disk containing data you no longer need. Do not use your Project Disk for this lesson, as all information on the disk will be erased.

Trouble?

This appendix assumes that the drive that will contain your floppy disks is drive A. If not, substitute the correct drive when you are instructed to use the 3½ Floppy (A:) drive.

1. Start your computer and **Windows XP** if necessary, then place a 3½-inch floppy disk in drive A

2. Double-click the **My Computer icon** 🖳 on the desktop

My Computer opens, as shown in Figure AP-1. This window lists all the drives and printers that you can use on your computer. Because computers have different drives, printers, programs, and other devices installed, your window will probably look different.

3. Right-click the **3½ Floppy (A:) icon**

When you click with the right mouse button, a shortcut menu of commands that apply to the item you right-clicked appears. Because you right-clicked a drive, the Format command is available.

Trouble?

Windows cannot format a disk if it is write-protected; therefore, you may need to slide the write-protect tab over until it clicks to continue. See Figure AP-3 to locate the write-protect tab on your disk.

4. Click **Format** on the shortcut menu

The Format dialog box opens, as shown in Figure AP-2. In this dialog box, you specify the capacity of the disk you are formatting, the File system, the Allocation unit size, the kind of formatting you want to do, and if you want, a volume label. You are doing a standard format, so you will accept the default settings.

5. Click **Start**, then, when you are warned that formatting will erase all data on the disk, click **OK** to continue

Windows formats your disk. After the formatting is complete, you might see a summary about the size of the disk.

6. Click **OK** when the message telling you that the format is complete appears, then click **Close** in the Format dialog box

QuickTip

Once a disk is formatted, you do not need to format it again. However, some people use the Quick Format option to erase the contents of a disk quickly, rather than having to select the files and then delete them.

7. Click the **Close button** ☒ in the My Computer window

My Computer closes and you return to the desktop.

FIGURE AP-1: **My Computer window**

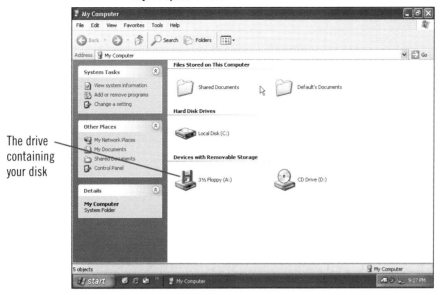

The drive
containing
your disk

FIGURE AP-2: **Format dialog box**

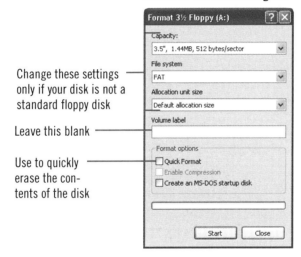

Change these settings
only if your disk is not a
standard floppy disk

Leave this blank

Use to quickly
erase the con-
tents of the disk

FIGURE AP-3: **Write-protect tab**

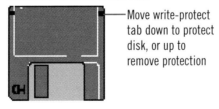

Move write-protect
tab down to protect
disk, or up to
remove protection

3.5" disk

More about disks

Disks are sometimes called **drives**, but this term really refers to the name by which the operating system recognizes the disk (or a portion of the disk). The operating system typically assigns a drive letter to a drive (which you can reassign if you want). For example, on most computers the hard disk is identified by the letter "C" and the floppy drive by the letter "A." The amount of information a disk can hold is called its capacity, usually measured in megabytes (MB). The most common floppy disk **capacity** is 1.44 MB. Computers also come with other disk drives, such as a **CD drives** and **Zip drives**. Such drives handle CDs and Zip disks, respectively. Both are portable like floppy disks, but they can contain far more data than floppy disks.

Glossary

Accessories Built-in programs that come with Windows XP.

Active program The program that you are using, differentiated from other open programs by a highlighted program button on the taskbar and a differently colored title bar.

Active window The window that you are currently using, differentiated from other open windows by a differently colored title bar.

Address bar The area below the toolbar in My Computer and Windows Explorer that you use to open and display a drive, folder, or Web page.

Back up To save files to another location in case you have computer trouble and lose files.

Browser A program, such as Microsoft Internet Explorer, designed to access the Internet.

Bullet mark A solid circle that indicates that an option is enabled.

Capacity The amount of information a disk can hold, usually measured in megabytes (MB).

Cascading menu A list of commands from a menu item with an arrow next to it; pointing to the arrow displays a submenu from which you can choose additional commands.

CD A disk that can contain programs, music, movies, or your own personal files. CDs can hold up to 700 MB of data.

CD drive A drive that can handle a CD.

Check box A square box in a dialog box that you click to turn an option on or off.

Check mark A mark that indicates that a feature is enabled.

Classic style A Windows XP setting in which you single-click to select items and double-click to open them.

Click To press and release the left mouse button once.

Clipboard A temporary storage space on your computer's hard disk containing information that has been cut or copied.

Close To quit a program or remove a window from the desktop. The Close button is usually located in the upper-right corner of a window.

Command A directive that provides access to a program's features.

Command button In a dialog box, a button that carries out an action. A command button usually has a label that describes its action, such as Cancel or Help. If the label is followed by an ellipsis (…), clicking the button displays another dialog box.

Context-sensitive help Help that is specifically related to what you are doing.

Control Panel A set of Windows XP tools used to change computer settings such as desktop colors or mouse settings.

Copy To place information onto the Clipboard in order to paste it in another location but also leave it in the original location.

Cut To remove information from a file and place it on the Clipboard, usually to be pasted into another location.

Default Settings preset by the operating system or program.

Delete To place a file or folder in the Recycle Bin, where you can either remove it from the disk permanently or restore it to its original location.

Desktop The screen that appears when you first start Windows XP, providing access to your computer's programs and files and to the Internet.

Dialog box A window that opens when more information is needed to carry out a command.

Document A file that you create using a program such as WordPad.

Double-click To press and release the left mouse button twice quickly.

Drag To move an item to a new location using the mouse.

Drive A device that reads and saves files on a disk and is also used to store files; floppy drives read and save files on floppy disks, whereas hard drives read and save files on your computer's built-in hard disk.

Edit To change the content or format of an existing file.

Explorer Bar The pane on the left side of the screen in Windows Explorer that lists all drives and folders on the computer.

File An electronic collection of information that has a unique name and location, distinguishing it from other files.

File hierarchy A logical structure for folders and files that mimics how you would organize files and folders in a filing cabinet.

File management The process of organizing and keeping track of files and folders.

Floppy disk A disk that you insert into a disk drive of your computer (usually drive A or B) to store files.

Folder An area on a disk that contains a collection of files and/or other folders that you use to help you organize your files.

Font The design of a set of characters (for example, Times New Roman).

Font size The size of text, measured in points (text that is one point is 1/72 inch tall).

Format To enhance the appearance of a document by, for example, changing the font or font size or adding borders and shading to a document. Also refers to the process of preparing a disk so it can store information.

Hard disk A disk that is built into the computer (usually drive C) on which you store files and programs.

Highlighting When an icon is shaded differently, indicating it is selected. *See also* Select.

Icon Graphical representation of computer elements such as files and programs.

Inactive Refers to a window or program that is open but not currently in use.

Input device An item such as a mouse or keyboard that you use to interact with your computer.

Insertion point A blinking vertical line that indicates where text will appear when you type.

Internet A worldwide collection of over 40 million computers linked together to share information.

Keyboard shortcut A keyboard alternative for executing a menu command (for example, [Ctrl][X] for Cut).

List box A box in a dialog box containing a list of items; to choose an item, click the list arrow, then click the desired item.

Maximize To enlarge a window so it fills the entire screen. The Maximize button is usually located in the upper-right corner of a window.

Menu A list of related commands in a program (for example, the File menu).

Menu bar A bar near the top of the program window that provides access to most of a program's features through categories of related commands.

Minimize To reduce the size of a window. The Minimize button is usually located in the upper-right corner of a window.

Mouse A handheld input device that you roll on your desk to position the mouse pointer on the Windows desktop. *See also* Mouse pointer.

Mouse buttons The buttons on the mouse (right and left, and sometimes a middle button or wheel) that you use to make selections and issue commands.

Mouse pointer The typically arrow-shaped object on the screen that follows the movement of the mouse. The shape of the mouse pointer changes depending on the program and the task being executed. *See also* Mouse.

Multi-tasking Working with more than one window or program at a time.

My Computer A program that you use to manage the drives, folders, and files on your computer.

Open To start a program or display a file.

Operating system A computer program that controls the basic operation of your computer and the programs you run on it. Windows XP is an example of an operating system.

Option button A small circle in a dialog box that you click to select an option.

Paint A graphics program that comes with Windows XP.

Pane A section of a divided window.

Pin To place a program on the upper-left part of the Start menu for quick access.

Point To position the mouse pointer in a particular location on your screen; also a unit of measurement (1/72 inch) used to specify the size of text.

Pointer trail A shadow of the mouse pointer that appears when you move the mouse (if you have the feature enabled); it helps you locate the pointer on your screen.

Program Task-oriented software that you use for a particular kind of work, such as word processing or database management. Microsoft Access, Microsoft Excel, and Microsoft Word are all programs.

Program button A button on the taskbar that represents an open program or window.

Properties Characteristics of a specific computer element (such as the mouse, keyboard, or desktop display) that you can customize.

Quick Launch toolbar A toolbar located next to the Start button on the taskbar that contains buttons to start Internet-related programs and to show the desktop.

Random access memory (RAM) The memory that programs use to perform necessary tasks while the computer is on. When you turn the computer off, all information in RAM is lost.

Recycle Bin A storage area on your computer's hard disk for deleted files, which remain in the Recycle Bin until you empty it. An icon on the desktop provides quick access to the Recycle Bin.

Restore To reduce the window to its size before it was maximized. The Restore button is usually located in the upper-right corner of a window.

Right-click To press and release the right mouse button once.

ScreenTip A description of a toolbar button that appears when you position the mouse pointer over the button.

Scroll bar A bar that appears at the bottom and/or right edge of a window whose contents are not entirely visible; you click the arrows or drag the box in the direction you want to move. *See also* Scroll box.

Scroll box A rectangle located in the vertical and horizontal scroll bars that indicates your relative position in a file and that you can drag to view other parts of the file or window. *See also* Scroll bar.

Select To highlight an item in order to perform some action on it. *See also* Highlighting.

Shortcut A link that you can place in any location that gives you quick access to a file, folder, or program located on your hard disk or network.

Shortcut menu A menu that appears when you right-click an item.

Shut down The action you perform when you have finished working with your computer; after you shut down it is safe to turn off your computer.

Slider An item in a dialog box that you drag to set the degree to which an option is in effect.

Spin box A box with two arrows and a text box; allows you to scroll in numerical increments or type a number.

Start button A button on the taskbar that you use to start programs, find and open files, access Windows Help and Support Center, and more.

Tab A place in a dialog box where related commands and options are organized.

Taskbar A strip at the bottom of the screen that contains the Start button, Quick Launch toolbar, and clock that shows buttons for the programs that are running.

Text box A rectangular area in a dialog box in which you type text.

Title bar The area along the top of the window that indicates the filename and program used to create it.

Toolbar A strip with buttons that allow you to activate a command quickly.

Web page A document located on another computer that you can view over the Internet and that often contains words, phrases, and graphics that link to other documents.

Web site A group of Web pages.

Window A rectangular frame on a screen that can contain icons, the contents of a file, and/or other usable data.

Windows Explorer A program that you use to manage files, folders, and shortcuts.

Windows Help and Support Center A resource that contains information about Windows XP and that includes an index, a table of contents, and links to useful Web pages.

WordPad A word-processing program that comes with Windows XP.

World Wide Web Part of the Internet that consists of Web pages located on different computers around the world.

Zip disk A portable disk that can contain 100 MB, far more than a regular floppy disk.

Zip drive A drive that can handle Zip disks.

Index

Index